Elite Nuggets

Your Handbook to Greatness

Dawud Ellayan

ISBN: 979-8-9887616-0-0

First Edition

Contents

Preface

I wrote this book after reading hundreds of books and research papers on personal development and techniques of high achievers in an effort to help people who are looking to master skills that are essential for professional and personal success. Although I don't claim to be an expert in any of these, I continue to add to my wealth of knowledge from anywhere I can find it, and if you are anything like me, you are too busy and don't have the time to read a 200-page book centered on a single idea with a lot of filler text and examples. That's why I focus on presenting techniques and ideas in this book with minimal fillers; everything is straight to the point! I use this as a reference for all the techniques that I know to keep my edge sharp, and I hope it does the same for you.

Let me start my book with this: Don't tell people your dreams, as their words might put you in a box of limitations based on their potential, not yours!

Time Management

Time management is an essential skill for life. Whoever you are, a student or a working professional, if you can't control your time, it will control you, which severely hinders your progress in this world. Numerous studies have shown that having time management skills lowers your stress and increases your job satisfaction, and it can also improve your health.[1] I think one of the best illustrations of the value of time comes from the 2011 movie *In Time*. The movie, which is classified as science fiction, depicts a future where people are biologically engineered to live for only one year once they reach age 25. In the movie, once a person hits 25 years of age, a clock on their arms will start counting down, and as time becomes a finite resource for people in the film, it becomes the primary source of currency. So, instead of getting paid for a job you do in dollars, you are paid in minutes that get added to your lifespan. Imagine living in a world where time is the most valuable re-

---

source—a place where time is more valuable than dollars, oil, silver, diamonds, and gold—so much so that you get paid in it! Well, guess what? We are already living in it; we just don't really know it! You see, we are already being paid for our time—we just use money as a proxy for it. All our jobs are defined by the amount of money per unit of time.

For example, let us take my friend John. He makes $20 per hour as a pharmacy tech in our local pharmacy. John is our go-to guy for parties. If you call him, he will always come and spend 5 hours with you partying, but if you ask him to lend you some cash, he is cheap as a goat. So, he will gladly give you 5 hours of his life, but not its equivalent in money. But please don't get me wrong, I'm not saying you must stop having any sort of fun. What I'm saying is we need to start looking at the true value of things because the government can always print more dollars, but no one can give you more time. We all only get 1,440 minutes in a day for God knows how many days, so we need to make the best use of it through time management skills.

On another note, poor time management skills can be detrimental to our overall well-being. Having poor time management skills can affect our ability to manage our work-life balance. Moreover, it can lead to poor productivity at work, with missed deadlines and lower life satisfaction.[2] So, developing our time (life) management skills should be a priority for all of us.

When we talk about time management, we can be talking either about long-term time management or short-term time management. Let's start by talking about long-term time management. This is the time management that you will be using to achieve your overall goal(s) in a year (or even longer). Short-term time management is what you will be using to get things done on a daily basis. Now it goes without saying that there wouldn't be any long-term time management if it's not built on a strong foundation, which is strong short-term time management.

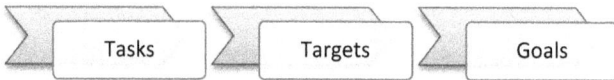

Tasks	Targets	Goals

So, now that we have established the importance of time management, let's look at how we can manage our time. I take a goal-oriented approach to time management, which follows the workflow depicted below; however, this can be applied wherever time management is needed:

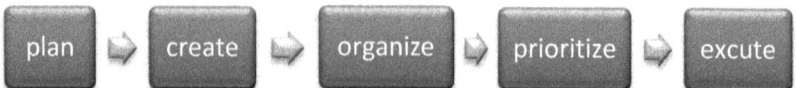

plan → create → organize → prioritize → excute

Plan

In this step, you need to jot down your goals, targets, and tasks (or brainstorm, if you don't know them yet) and aim to accurately capture your available free time to work on those tasks per day. To elaborate, a target is an objective that needs to be reached to achieve your goal, whereas tasks are the things that are needed to achieve the targets. For example, let's say that you want to buy a house at the end of this year, and we are currently in January. That would be your goal, while your target would be to get a certain amount of money each month to reach your goal. And finally, your tasks will be the things that you do on a day-to-day basis to reach your target each month. If you're having trouble getting started, you can use the 5 Ws and 3 Hs method illustrated in the figure below to help you get started with brainstorming ideas and learning to capture those ideas.

First, start by asking yourself what your goal is. What do you need to achieve it? Be specific as much as you can. What is your timeline? But don't just think about it, write your thoughts down in your goal bucket. Using our previous example, your goal would be to buy a new house, your timeline would be a year, and what you need to get it done is more money. But, remember to be specific. So, instead of just saying "more money," state the amount needed. So, let's say you need $100K.

Second, we need to look at our targets per our timeline. In our example, that would be $100K divided by 12 months, or $8,333/month. If you can save $2,000 a month from your current job, your monthly target would be to get an extra $6,333, which leads us to the how. Well, you can look for a second job, start investing, … Etc.

And that brings us to our building blocks, "our tasks" that we need to do to get to our targets. Let's say we decided to work in a delivery service on the side to accomplish our target. This will be our goal-oriented task that needs to be incorporated into our daily schedule along with our regular day-to-day tasks. Our final step would be to figure out how much time each task needs to be completed and how much free time we have to begin with.

Goal
- What is it?
- What do you need to get it done?
- What is your time-line?

Targets
- How can it be done?
- How long does it take to complete?

Tasks
- What are they?
- What do you need to get them done?
- How much time does each task take?

Create

In the "create" step, we need to look at what we wrote down in the previous step and fill in our plan portfolio as depicted in Table-1 or arrange it in a similar manner using a different tool to help us capture everything in an organized manner. The goal of this step is to get an organized overview of your activity portfolio to better understand where you stand and provide the groundwork to organize your schedule in the next step.

Table-1						
Goal	Targets		Task		Day	Hours available
	Target	Time needed	Task	Time needed	Saturday	
					Sunday	
					Monday	
					Tuesday	
					Wednesday	
					Thursday	
					Friday	

Organize

In this step, we need to incorporate what we have already identified as targets and tasks in our previous steps into the available time. However, this doesn't mean that we go and start making to-do lists, as more than 40% of all to-do lists never get completed.[3] Rather, it means scheduling calendar appointments for each task so that you have a specified time to complete a task. You can think of it as a commitment with yourself so that no other thing can be done within that specified time, as it is already spoken for.

Now, one of the biggest mistakes people make when they get to this point is trying to cram as much as possible into a short period of time or to try to get through a big task in one sitting that actually requires multiple hours. You are bound to get distracted, and your productivity will go down, as after all, we are humans, not machines! And that can cause you to feel bad because you couldn't do what you had scheduled. So, instead, break down the work into manageable chunks and use the Pomodoro Technique to space them out. The Pomodoro Technique was created by Francesco Cirillo to boost productivity and increase concentration. The technique suggests allocating 25 minutes for each task. You can apply this method by adding tasks on your calendar in 30-minute intervals and setting up a timer for 25 minutes when you start the task. Once the 25 minutes are up, you would rest for 5 minutes before moving on to the next task or resuming with the same one. This will help program your mind to devote its full attention to the task at hand during these 25 minutes, as it creates a fake sense of urgency that will work to enhance your attention. Moreover, you won't be distracted by looking at the clock every few moments to see if it is time to take a break.

However, more important than the "25 minutes" is the principle behind it, which is the use of a timer that can help us increase our productivity and make the best use of our time. For example, part of my morning routine is what I call a 5-10 hour. Every day from 6 am to 7 am, I do 5 tasks, with 10 minutes assigned for each task; first, I read 10 minutes of the Quran (for my mind and soul), next I read 10 minutes of a book (for my mind and personal development), and then I do 10 minutes of learning Spanish through Duolingo. Afterward, I read a book related to my job (helping keep my information current), then I exercise for 10 minutes (for my body). If you are wondering what kind of exercise you can do in 10 minutes, well I repeat a circle of 10 pushups, 10 squats, and 10 sit-ups until time runs out, and believe me, it does the job! Then, the remaining 10 minutes are for rest, in which I have my breakfast and head to work. Let me tell you—those 10-minute tasks add up like compound interest, and I always feel up for doing them, as they are just 10 minutes! So, with this 5-10 method, you can change your life just 10 minutes at a time!

Prioritize

How to prioritize your tasks is one of the most important skills you'll ever develop! In the words of Stephen Covey, you need to "put first things first." After all, 20% of the work you do is responsible for 80% of results, as noted by the Italian economist Vilfredo Pareto, which was later known as the Pareto Principle or the 80/20 rule. Pareto came up with this principle after noticing that 80% of the land in Italy was owned by 20% of the population. And the same goes for most activities to a certain degree. As such, we need to determine the activities that produce the best outcomes for us, concentrate on them, and drop the others. This brings us to two tools that can help us prioritize our work and improve our efficiency.

DDR

DDR stands for "Drop, Delegate, and Redesign." Three questions were developed by Harvard professors Birkinshaw and Cohen in 2013 that can save you eight hours of desk work and meetings every week.[4]

1. Drop. What can I completely stop doing?
2. Delegate. What can be delegated or outsourced?
3. Redesign. What process needs to be changed? How can a process be improved?

Ask yourself these questions at the start of every week and every new venture, as they will force your mind to think outside of the box, which will ultimately improve your work efficiency through better time utilization.

Eisenhower Box

The Eisenhower Box is named for Dwight D. Eisenhower, Supreme Commander of the Allied Expeditionary Force in Europe during World War II and the 34th president of the United States. Eisenhower was always incredibly organized. His productivity strategy, the Eisenhower Box (or Eisenhower Matrix) is an easy-to-use tool to help you prioritize your work.

Eisenhower Box	Urgent	Not urgent
Important	Urgent and important: Do it now • _____ • _____	Important, but not urgent: schedule a time to do it. • _____ • _____
Not important	Urgent but not important: Delegate. • _____ • _____	Not important and not urgent: Drop it. • _____ • _____

Execute

Now that we have our schedule planned, it is time to execute it! Plans without actions are just daydreams. Proper execution is integral to the success of any project. Consistently sticking to the schedule and acting on it is crucial to success. That is why you need to learn to say no to pop-up meetings and other distractions unless they are truly necessary. A meeting should have an agenda and a clear goal. Data from 1,000+ workers show that 71% of meetings are a waste of time,[5] so protect your time and don't be afraid to say no to meetings!

Now let's talk about multitasking. Multitasking is always raved about as being a good thing, but it actually reduces comprehension, attention, and overall cognitive performance.[6] So, how can you stop multitasking and avoid distractions when you are working on an important project? Well, one method that is helpful for short-term tasks is the OHIO principle, which stands for "Only Handle It Once." The notion behind this principle is that once you begin working on a certain activity, you do it until completion without interruption. For instance, following the OHIO principle, if you get an email while working on a task, either work on the email until completion if urgent or flag it for later without wasting any time or attention on it. One way to accomplish this is by scheduling a time to process emails every day and only look at emails during this time.

For example, set up a calendar appointment for 15 or 30 minutes to look at emails at 8 a.m. and 2 p.m. every day. This way, you can reserve your focus for the tasks at hand and not worry about missing an important email.

On another note, this brings me to a much-needed change in our culture regarding the writing of email subject lines.

Compose subject lines efficiently so that they contain information regarding the urgency of the email and expectations for a response. This can also help minimize the stress of missing out on emails and the need to take more than one look at each email.

Leadership

L eadership is a great skill to have, and it is essential to the success of any team, family, or company. Great leadership spans all domains of life, and great leaders are capable of raising morale, uniting their people, and achieving their goals. Moreover, a leader is someone who is reliable in times of need—someone you can lean on when times get tough. As such, great leaders have to be strong and resilient because you can't lean on a weak wall—it will crumble! On another note, there is a misconception that we need to clear up before we dive into what it takes to become a great leader. A lot of people would associate leaders with authoritative figures like managers, military commanders, and so on. Yes, if you are in a position of authority, you need to have great leadership skills to be successful. However, you do not need authority to be a leader! You can always lead without authority. For example, look at Greta Thunberg, an environmental activist, who at the age of 15 began to rally millions and challenge world leaders to mitigate climate change. Having the right leadership skill is like holding a flame in the darkest night. It will make people gravitate toward you and look up to you regardless of whether you have authority or not. On another note, you can't lead people without leading yourself first! As Bill George states, "The hardest person you will ever lead is yourself." Great leaders start by leading themselves first, so they feel confident in their own abilities and are comfortable in their own skin. They aren't concerned with self-promotion or getting credit. Rather, they are self-driven, and they understand that serving the organization, or the people, is the core principle of leadership. They view their leadership position as stewardship rather than ownership. So, let's talk about the skills and techniques that will light your flame.

To be a great leader you need:

1. Focus
2. Trust
3. Self-Accountability
4. Planning
5. Empowerment
6. Knowledge

Focus

Leaders must be laser-focused on their organization's goals. So, your first step would be to write down your organization or company goals and your mission statement and place it somewhere visible. Having your goals written and visible will keep them foremost in your mind and help center your focus around activities that lead to the accomplishment of those goals. Furthermore, being focused and having your goals written down will prevent derailment from the target as time goes by. To clarify this concept using a personal example, I have a friend who wants to lose weight badly, so each year on New Year's, he tells us, "I'm going to exercise and lose weight this year, I'm going to become the best version of myself." But he never writes anything down. Then, March comes around and his memory is foggy on what his goal truly was, and now his goal is simply to diet and lose a few pounds. You see, his goal got diluted with time because it wasn't written down.

You can scale up this example to anything! This brings up another point, which is that the written down goals must be as specific as possible to avoid false achievements. For instance, let's say a company's goal is to increase profits through revenue over the next year. If this goal is not written down, it can easily turn into increasing profit through cost reduction. So, at the end of the year, the numbers will match your goals, but the way you got those numbers won't match the actual goal, which was to increase profits through increased revenue. And you might be thinking to yourself, "What's wrong with that?" Well, first off, it is not the goal that you set out to achieve. Second, this false achievement might cover up a bigger underlying problem that is preventing the achievement of the set goal, and since the goal was achieved in other ways, no one will do a deeper dive into root cause analysis regarding why the original method didn't work. To go back to our previous example, this year, the profits hit the goal through cutting costs, but what will you do next year if you can't figure out why sales aren't increasing? You can't keep cutting costs, as that is not sustainable, and you have wasted a couple of years putting on Band-Aids instead of fixing the root cause.

Finding your passion and purpose for leadership goes beyond focusing on the organization's goal. You also need to find the balance between your intrinsic and extrinsic motivations. Extrinsic motivation would be, say, the desire to get promoted, get a pay raise, and so on, whereas intrinsic motivation is about getting that internal satisfaction and happiness that comes from reaching for a great purpose. Extrinsic motivation can be found at any job and with any role, but intrinsic motivation is what people have a hard time discovering. That's because we never take the time to sit down and think about it. So, take some time and figure out why you are in the business you are, because your extrinsic motivation will run out one day, but your intrinsic motivation will never run out. It will keep you going despite all the hardships that you may face as a leader. One way to start thinking about your intrinsic motivation is by remembering that leadership's true purpose is to serve; so, think about who you are serving and whose lives you are making better. Why do you need to make your organization better? Answers to those questions will help you find your motivation. Finally, although I place a greater emphasis on intrinsic motivation, finding a balance between the two is an ideal way to go, as one sustains the other in the long run and both are needed to live a happy, fulfilled life as a leader.

Trust

Leadership without trust is a coup waiting to happen! For you to lead, the people that you're leading need to trust you fully or they will not follow you with all their intent. On the other hand, you need to fully trust the people you manage to avoid micromanaging them. After all, to be successful, you need everyone in your organization to be fully present, at ease in their own skins, and confident in their own abilities. Establishing an atmosphere of trust is of vital importance for great leaders, as we tend to present our true selves around the people that we trust the most.

So, how can leaders establish trust with their teams?

First, respect among team members and leaders is of vital importance and is the basis of any healthy relationship. In the words of Albert Einstein, "Everyone should be respected as an individual, but no one idolized." Mutual respect keeps the dialog open, and no one will be afraid to be themself if they have the respect of their peers and leaders. To respect your team means valuing their opinions rather than diminishing them.

Second, leaders should interact with their teams with empathy. To interact with empathy is the ability to understand where the other person is coming from, the ability to put yourself in someone else's shoes. Furthermore, empathic leaders are comfortable with themselves, so they are more open to sharing their vulnerabilities, which builds and strengthens ties and connections among team members. Interaction with empathy will provide a psychologically safe place that addresses emotional needs that will give freedom of expression to everyone without fear of repercussions.

Finally, if you trust your team, you will feel more comfortable delegating responsibilities to them, which will further create an environment in which everyone is a leader in their own domain. So, it moves the conversation from leader-follower into leader-leader, which is far more effective. Moreover, treating everyone with respect fosters an inclusive environment versus an exclusive one. After all, relationships count more than the structure for workforce sustainability.

Self-Accountability

Great leaders hold themselves and their teams to the highest standards. Gaining self-awareness is the first step to holding yourself accountable and to extreme ownership, as presented by Jocko Willink. To clarify, you should have the awareness and presence of mind to own up to your errors and your teams' errors, as well. We all make mistakes; however, how we react to those mistakes is what separates great leaders from lousy ones. Great leaders are not afraid to take ownership of errors that happen under their watch rather than quickly looking for a scapegoat to take the blame, which is what lousy leaders do. Instead, a great leader will not react emotionally but will accept the error, find the reason why it happened, and try to prevent it from happening again. For example, let's say you manage a major real estate firm, and one of your staff members failed to update your list of new houses on the market, which led to your marketing department forgetting to run ads for those new houses. Now sales are down, but you have figured out the problem. How does accepting accountability come into play in this scenario? Well, you can yell and penalize the employee who made the error, or you can have the self-awareness to see that the root cause of the error might be the company's SOPs (standard operating procedures) relating to how new listings get updated and posted. Furthermore, this approach will make all employees feel safe and supported by their leadership.

The best way to show self-accountability to your team is to communicate through action. As the saying goes, you need to practice what you preach, for not doing so will hurt your credibility. For example, my grandpa is a 30+ year smoker. I took him to the doctor one time, and the doc was telling him that he needs to stop smoking, as his health is deteriorating. So, my grandpa nodded his head, and he proceeded to light up a cigarette as soon as we were out of the door! I said, "You just nodded your head that you will quit smoking. What are you doing?" And he responded, "I saw that doctor smoking, as well, and if it was as bad as he says, he wouldn't be doing it!" So, despite the overwhelming evidence against smoking, the fact that the doctor is just talking the talk without walking the walk stopped my grandpa from following his advice. Interestingly, more than 20% of physicians smoke,[7] so you can only imagine how many patients feel the same way as my grandpa, which highlights the importance of holding yourself accountable and practicing what you preach!

Lastly, in order to be self-accountable and keep yourself in check, you need to define your ethical boundaries, which brings us to the *New York Times Test*, a tool leaders can use to define their ethical limits. Before acting, consider how you would feel if the *New York Times* published the details of what you are doing, including the transcripts of the conversations you will have had. If this causes you to feel bad, it's time to reconsider what you're doing. On the other side, if you feel good about it, you should feel free to continue, even if others disagree with your choices.[8]

Planning

Great leaders are great planners. To be a great planner, you need to do three things: anticipate, simplify, and act. First of all, the ability to anticipate outcomes can mean the difference between success and failure. Imagining the future will fill you with hope and curiosity and might help you predict the future because if you can imagine what can go wrong, you can plan for it and be better prepared to deal with it if it happens. On the other hand, if you can predict the success of your plan, you can also try coming up with better ways to do it, or perhaps decide not to do it at all if the result you imagine is not worth the trouble. Second, great planners can simplify their dreams; they can set small goals to gauge big dreams. As the Chinese proverb goes, "The journey of a thousand miles begins with a single step." All big goals can be simplified into smaller goals that can help you achieve those goals. Great planners should have the ability to simplify their end goal into smaller targets that fit into an action plan.

One way you can simplify your goal is by continuing to ask yourself, "How can I do that?" For example, let's say you want to achieve goal "A." Start by asking yourself how you can achieve goal "A." Well, by doing "B" and "C." And how you get to "B" and C" is by doing "D," and so on. To clarify, you know your goal, "point A," and you know where you stand, "point D." All you have to do is figure out the path of getting from "D" to "A" by continuing to ask yourself "how?" But don't do it verbally; write it all down. Finally, a plan with no action is like playing basketball without the ball. It is just a daydream! A great plan is only great if followed by great action, so it is up to leaders to take initiative and implement the plan!

Empowerment

Empowering is probably one of the most common characteristics of great leaders. People tend to remember those who empowered them and gave them the freedom and the tools to be successful. Examples of famous leaders who empower their teams are Steve Jobs and Warren Buffet. This empowering style of leadership is also known as the laissez-faire or delegative leadership approach, which is based on recognizing your teams' talents and strengths and delegating the work to them based on those attributes. In other words, you will empower your team through extra responsibilities that bring out their unique qualities, which will promote excellence and encourage growth in any environment. Hence, this approach will lead to increased accountability, lower stress, and improved job satisfaction. As team members are delegated a responsibility, they become the leaders for that responsibility, which will facilitate a leader-leader communication style that promotes trust and respect among team members. Moreover, delegating certain tasks will give you, as a leader, more time to work on what matters most. But, before delegating responsibilities, you need to recognize your team's strengths first or you will be delegating responsibilities to people who can't handle them! So, start by knowing your team members and their strengths, then move on to delegating responsibilities to them accordingly.

Knowledge

As the saying goes, "Knowledge is power," and those who hold this power are bound to lead and take control of a situation. In other words, only people who know what to do will do. And leaders know what needs to be done and how to get from A to B. Furthermore, teams expect their leaders to get more done, be available 24/7, and respond as if all the information is always at their fingertips.

Here, it's important to differentiate between three types of knowledge needed by leaders, which can be summarized with the following three questions:

Question #1: Who are you leading? Knowing your team members and their strengths and weaknesses is very important, as it can help you distribute the work and delegate activities based on those attributes. Moreover, knowing your team's weaknesses helps you provide the ultimate support to them. Lastly, it is important to note that knowing your team members starts by knowing yourself first and acknowledging to yourself your strengths and weaknesses. As stated before, self-awareness is a vital skill for leaders.

Question #2: Why are you leading? What is the purpose of your leadership? Understanding your leadership goal will help shape your day-to-day activities. Furthermore, it will serve as a compass that guides your focus toward goal achievement. In other words, you won't know the right path to take if you don't know where you are going!

Question #3: How? This refers to functional and operational knowledge in the workplace. First, there is functional knowledge, which is basically knowing how the job is done, and this is usually the technical knowledge you would learn through experience and training. Second, operational knowledge covers how to deal with issues, stress, and conflict. Although functional knowledge is important, I would argue that operational knowledge is far more significant. For instance, think of the McDonald's story as depicted in the movie *The Founder*. Even though the two brothers who actually started the company had the functional knowledge, they eventually lost the company to a man who had far more operational knowledge than they did once he capitalized on their functional knowledge.

Two Important Parts of Operational Knowledge

So, let's talk about two important parts of operational knowledge: problem-solving and communication skills.

#1. Problem-Solving

How to problem solve is one of the greatest operational skills a leader can have. Because guess what? There are always going to be problems, as all roads to success are paved with them. So, as leaders, we need to know how to deal with issues without losing track of our goals. Whenever a problem is encountered, you need to learn to take a step back and identify the most central issue; by doing that, you are almost halfway to a solution.

A problem is only as big as you make it. If you see it as

a big problem, you will only make it bigger. Instead, break it down into smaller pieces as much as possible and then tackle one piece at a time. Dissecting a problem into smaller pieces reduces stress and can help identify the root cause of the issue. As such, it can help direct your efforts into the piece with the greatest potential effect.

So, how can we dissect a problem into bite size pieces? Two great methods are the Yes/No tree and the 5 Whys.

The Yes/No Tree

First, the Yes/ No Tree. In this method, you start with a subject and then proceed down the tree using a series of Yes/No questions to help guide the flow of your thinking. The great thing about the Yes/No Tree is that it can be turned into a standard operating procedure for your team when encountering specific problems, which will improve efficiency by resolving issues systematically and quickly. For instance, if you have ever experienced an issue with your internet and had to call your provider, they usually ask you a series of yes/no questions to help you troubleshoot the problem using their premade yes/no tree (see the example below). There are plenty of templates online that can be used, and they are applicable in numerous situations and job fields.

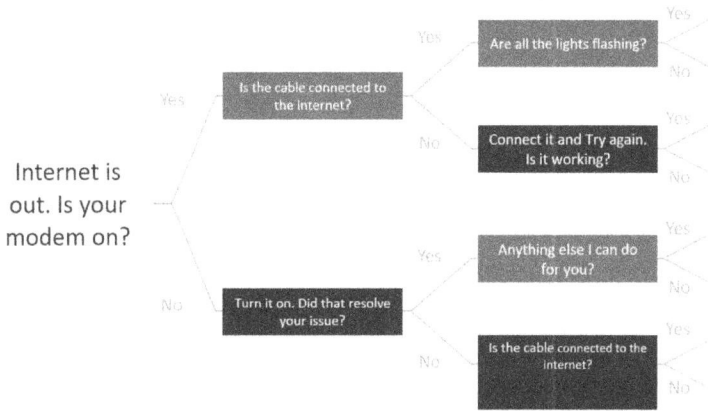

Although the Yes/No Tree is a great tool for trouble-shooting issues, using it for identification of root cause analysis might not be practicable when a clear flow of the process and a list of the common issues don't exist, which brings us to our second method: the 5 Whys.

The 5 Whys

The 5 Whys method works great to identify the root cause of an issue, and it can be applied on an individual or team level. The way it works is that you need to ask why 5 times until the root cause is identified. Individually, you can start asking yourself why 5 times to identify the root cause through the following structure:

1. Why did "A" happen?

    Answer: Because of "B"

2. Why did "B" happen?

    Answer: Because of "C"

3. Why did "C" happen?

    Answer: Because of "D"

4. Why did "D" happen?

    Answer: Because of "E"

5. Why did "E" happen?

    Answer: Because of "F"

So, what is the root cause for "A"? "F." To further clarify this, let's say that the issue at hand is that you are late for work.

1. Why were you late for work?

    There was traffic.

2. Why was there traffic?

    I usually leave at 6:30, but today I left at 7 a.m., and I got caught in rush hour traffic.

3. Why did you leave at 7 a.m.?

    I missed my alarm.

4. Why did you miss your alarm?

    My phone died on me, so it didn't ring.

5. Why did your phone battery die on you?

    I forgot to check its charge before I went to sleep.

So, the root cause in this case was forgetting to check the phone charge before going to sleep, and the solution is to set up a system of checking the phone charge before going to sleep.

On the other hand, teams can also use the 5 Whys method coupled with brainstorming where the entire team contributes to the answers for each question and votes on each answer as they move down the five questions flow until a root cause is identified. The only difference between the application on the individual level versus the team level is that team members will need to vote on each response. As such, they will follow the following structure:

1 Why did "A" happen?

   Answer: Because of "B," "C," or "D."

   Coming up with different answers is expected in brainstorming sessions, and in this case, you will have the team vote on what the most likely answer is. If, after voting, the team is torn between two options, then the wisest approach is to divide the team into two groups, explore each option separately, and then regroup after the end of the 5 Whys to see if there is a connection down the line between the options. Furthermore, this would allow us to explore all the viable options at one time.

However, caution is warranted to not explore so many options that the team's effort and concentration are wasted by dividing the team into numerous groups.

2. Why did "B" or "C" happen? Each group will separately examine why "B" happened or why "C" happened.

   Answer: After a vote, because of "E."

3. Why did "E" happen?

   Answer: After a vote, because of "F."

4. Why did "G" happen?

   Answer: After a vote, because of "Y."

5. Why did "Y" happen?

   Answer: After a vote, because of "X."

#2. Communication Skills

Great communication skills are vital to a leader's success. First, communication skills are necessary for leaders to be able to relay their ideas and goals clearly to their teams. After all, if your crew doesn't know what they have to do, they won't do it! Second, good communication is essential to build trust between you and your team, which is of vital importance as discussed earlier in this chapter. On the other hand, good communication is as much about listening as it is about talking. And listening is as important a skill as any, especially for a coaching style of leadership.

A coaching style of leadership, as the name implies, involves approaching your leadership position as a coach to your team, a leader that aims to inspire their team members to do their best and help them see their job as much more than just a paycheck but also as an opportunity for personal and professional growth. Furthermore, as a coach, you should be setting up SMART goals (specific, measurable, attainable, relevant, and time-based) for your team and setting up points along their timeline to meet and discuss your team's progress toward those goals.

As such, one-on-one conversations are essential for the success of this style of leadership. This is the best time for a coach to learn about their team's personalities, goals, and, more importantly, the challenges they are experiencing. By providing an emotionally and physically safe space for discussion, you will facilitate honest dialog that will bring any issues to the surface. Don't forget that your team is on the frontlines dealing with issues day in and day out, and if they fear the repercussions of speaking up, they are unlikely to mention anything to you, especially if you are contributing to the issue. Hence, you will lose out on receiving feedback that might be important for your career as a leader. Also, this time will be ideal for you to give feedback to your team members. Truly, giving honest and productive feedback is as vital for their success as it is for yours. However, there are a few things to note here, as giving feedback is a skill in itself.

First, giving positive feedback is more important than giving negative feedback, as it will help frame the listener's mind in a more positive way. So, a general rule of thumb is that for every negative feedback, there should be two positive feedbacks about what was done well. Moreover, you should attempt to reframe the feedback as an opportunity for growth and development. As coach and author Marshall Goldsmith puts it, we should view feedback as feedforward. You should view this time as an opportunity to promote excellence and improve productivity rather than as a disciplinary session. Furthermore, any dispute should be viewed as a difference of opinion that should be approached with an argument based on sound logic rather than an emotional battle to show who is right. Additionally, be open to contrary opinions and actively listen to the points being made so you can logically assess them and give feedback accordingly. Whenever an issue is encountered, as a coach, your duty will be to guide the person's thinking by carefully listening and asking leading questions. For example, posing questions like, "How do you think that went?" and "How could you have done that differently?" will help reframe the mindset of your listener from being under investigation to being a partner in the solution. Communication is a vital skill for leaders, as proper communication is essential for relaying ideas and resolving conflicts.

Mentorship

This chapter is for anyone who wants to be a mentor or wants to be a mentee. You see, mentorship is a two-way street. While a mentor is responsible for providing guidance and support, the mentee must also be open to feedback, actively seek out opportunities for growth, and take responsibility for their own development. To make a mentor relationship work, both parties must be committed to the process and willing to put in the time and effort required. For those willing to invest in mentorship, the rewards can be substantial, both personally and professionally. One of the most important advantages of mentorship is the chance for the mentee to learn from the mentor's experiences and mistakes. A mentor can help you avoid common pitfalls and develop a more subtle understanding of your field by sharing their own stories and lessons learned. Although mentors can help support you in understanding how much hard work is needed to be successful, they should also challenge you and your way of thinking, as what you learn through such challenging is far superior to what you will learn in any other way.

Mentoring can take many different forms, ranging from formal programs within an organization to informal relationships between individuals. For example, a mentor can help a mentee build their network and connect with other professionals in their field, in addition to providing guidance and support. This is especially useful for people who are just starting out in their careers, as building a strong network is often necessary for success. On the other hand, if you are a father or a mother, you have to be a mentor for your kids, showing them the right way to do things and how to avoid your past mistakes so history doesn't repeat itself. Whatever the structure, effective mentoring requires a few key components; availability, knowledge, and communication skills.

First, a mentor must have and be willing to put time and effort into this relationship. A strong mentor-mentee relationship takes time and effort, and a mentor must be invested in their mentee's development and growth. Second, a mentor must possess the knowledge and experience necessary to provide valuable guidance to their mentee, which may result from years of experience in a specific industry, a specific area of expertise, or simply a thorough understanding of what it takes to be successful in a specific field. Finally, a mentor must be an effective communicator and listener. Effective mentoring necessitates open and honest communication, as well as the ability to provide constructive and supportive feedback.

While mentorship is generally thought of as a relationship between two people where a mentor is someone who guides, advises, and supports a mentee by sharing their expertise and knowledge to help the mentee reach their full potential, the best mentor can actually come in the form of a book! As Al-Mutanabbi (an Arabic poet) once said, "The most dignified place on earth is a steed's saddle, and **the best companion through time is a book.**" Books have long been regarded as one of the most effective sources of mentorship. While a mentor can provide tailored advice and support, books provide a wealth of knowledge and wisdom that can be accessed at any time and from any location. Below are a few examples of how books can be excellent mentors and provide an advantage over traditional mentors.

First of all, books can provide inspiration. Reading about other people's experiences and accomplishments can be extremely motivating and inspiring. Moreover, books can give readers the tools and strategies they need to achieve their own goals and pursue their interests.

Second, books can offer a wide range of perspectives. Unlike an individual mentor, who may have a specific point of view or bias, books provide a diverse range of perspectives and insights from various authors and experts, which can help readers gain a more comprehensive understanding of a specific topic or issue. However, I have to stress that this would only work if you read books by different authors on the same topic, not books by a single author. As in the latter, you would just be reaffirming the same point of view of that author rather than being exposed to a diverse range of perspectives.

Third, books offer flexibility, as they provide for self-paced learning. Truly, books, unlike mentors, can be read and studied at the reader's leisure, which allows readers to take their time digesting the information and applying it to their own lives. Furthermore, books can be revisited and referred to at any time. Unlike a mentor, who may move on or retire, books can be revisited and referred to over and over again. As they continue to grow and develop, readers can refresh their knowledge and gain new insights as their perspective changes with time and experience.

Fourth, books offer accessibility, as they are often more affordable and accessible than traditional mentors. While some mentorship programs can be costly or time-consuming, and access to mentors might not be feasible unless they work in the same company, etc., books are relatively inexpensive and available to anyone with a library card or an internet connection.

Of course, books cannot fully substitute for personalized mentorship, as there are numerous advantages to working directly with a mentor. However, books can be an extremely valuable source of guidance, knowledge, and inspiration for those who are unable to find a mentor or prefer to work independently.

Productivity

Productivity refers to our capacity to carry out tasks and accomplish goals effectively and efficiently. We talked in an earlier chapter about time management and how it is essential for productivity, and in this chapter, we will discuss more techniques to help boost productivity.

The Power of Positive Thinking

The philosophy of positive thinking is based on the notion that a person's thoughts and attitudes have a significant impact on their surroundings and their quality of life. In general, it involves the practice of focusing on positive thoughts, beliefs, and attitudes while trying to eradicate negative ones. One of the key principles of positive thinking is that our thoughts create our reality, which means that how we experience a situation or event depends on how we frame it in our minds. For example, if we approach a difficult task with a negative attitude, we are more likely to struggle and possibly fail. On the other hand, if we approach the same task with a positive attitude, we are more likely to be fully present and engaged. Hence, we will be more efficient, and we are more likely to achieve our goal. Additionally, positive thinking can help us overcome productivity barriers, such as procrastination. We are more inclined to begin a task when we can concentrate on the benefits of completing it. In other words, you are more likely to start walking into a tunnel if you can see the light at the end of it. Thus, having the foresight to see the end result, "the light at the end of the tunnel," will help us avoid procrastination and other types of resistance that may prevent us from achieving our goals.

Positive thinking can boost our productivity by helping us maintain a positive work-life balance. By adopting a positive mindset and focusing on the positive aspects of our work, we can boost our confidence and stay focused and engaged at work. Moreover, our physical health, which is vital for productivity, can be greatly impacted by positive thoughts. For instance, positive thinkers are more likely to recover faster from illnesses and injuries and are less likely to have stress-related diseases, such as heart disease and high blood pressure.[9] On another note, positive thinking can help us develop strong, healthy relationships, as we have a better chance of developing solid, enduring relationships when we approach others with a positive attitude and an open mind. We are more likely to feel content and happy when we focus on the positive aspects of our relationships. Consequently, having good physical health and a strong support system (due to robust and healthy relationships) will result in a great foundation for peak performance and productivity.

Now that we have gone through some of the benefits of positive thinking for productivity, let's talk about how we can develop and nourish a positive-thinking mindset:

First, always remember that you can control what you put into the world, but you can't control the outcome. So, don't worry about the result as long as you are on the right path!

Second, practice gratitude. By concentrating on the blessings in our lives, we can divert our attention from a negative mindset to a more positive one, which will develop a sense of contentment.

Third, practice positive self-talk. Your brain listens to what you say to it, so be kind to yourself! For instance, if you keep saying, "I have a bad memory," guess what? You will start to develop a bad memory. A good rule of thumb is to treat your self-talk as if you were talking to your best friend! Imagine that you are giving your best friend advice. How would you do it? Would you be rude and inconsiderate, or would you be nice and try not to hurt their feelings because you hold their best interest at heart? If you are a good friend, your answer would be the latter. So, why treat people better than you treat yourself? You are your own original best friend; act like it! On the other hand, you shouldn't be too quick to accept what people say as truth when it comes to your potential, as people will often try to define your reach based on their abilities. That doesn't mean that you shouldn't accept feedback and advice, but you shouldn't let that advice and feedback define you!

Fourth, find something to smile about every day when you wake up and when you go to bed. This is a great habit to have because it will train your brain to be happy. With time, this habit will help you find happiness in the smallest things throughout the day. After all, if you are happy, you are more likely to enter a state of flow and to be more focused and productive.

Fifth, compete with yourself, not with others. If you compare yourself to other people, you will never win for two main reasons. In the first place, we all have limited mental bandwidth that gets used up by our activities throughout the day. Hence, monitoring the success of others is adding another activity that meaninglessly drains your mental energy. So, don't let it happen, and reserve your mental energy for the things that truly matter. Truly, your goal should always be to compete with yourself and be the best version of yourself, not others.

Have you ever heard the phrase "the greatest of all time," aka "GOAT"? It is a commonly used phrase nowadays, and I'm here to tell you there is no such thing! No matter how great a person is, there is always someone greater! Consequently, you shouldn't try to be greater than others because there will always be someone greater than you. So, just try to be the greatest version of yourself! Don't worry about where you rank, because ego is dangerous, and I don't think there is a worse trait to have than being egotistical! If you think you are the greatest, you will stop looking for ways to improve and will stop listening to people's advice. As the Chinese proverb goes, "Empty your cup," because you can't fill an already full cup. To elaborate, your mind is the cup in this case, and it is full of ideas. If it thinks it is at maximum capacity, it is not going to receive anymore.

Sixth, failure is inevitable. You can't succeed at everything, but you can't let the fear of failure stop you from trying to succeed. Embracing the potential of failure as a learning opportunity will free your mind from worrying so that it can focus instead on doing. For example, a lot of people won't start their own business, even though they daydream about it nearly every day, because they think their business will fail. Well guess what, there is a great chance it would, but having that fear from the beginning won't just prevent you from getting started, but it will also limit your potential for creativity. Instead of thinking about "how to be innovative," your mindset will be focused on "how to stop the business from failing." The latter is a productivity mind trap, as you may think you are productive by "not failing," but, in fact, you are just merely existing. So, don't let fear of failure define your success. Embrace it as the learning opportunity it is, and your productivity will peak.

Seventh, small wins are important. No matter what your goal in life is, having small wins throughout is important, as those small wins will help shift and maintain your mindset in a more positive spectrum. I recommend you listen to Admiral William H. McRaven's speech delivered at the 2014 Commencement of the University of Texas. In it, the admiral asserts that if you want to change the world, you have to start by making your bed every morning. The point is that if you make your bed every morning, that will be your first win of the day, and small as it is, this win will prime your mind for success. So, start your day with a win, and make your bed!

Focus

Focus is essential for productivity. For me, being focused is all about being in a state of "flow," the state in which my brain is so completely engaged in a pleasantly challenging activity that I lose track of time. I so thoroughly enjoy it that once I finish a day's work, I can't wait to get back in it! After all, getting to a state of flow is natural for our brains. But we get so overwhelmed with life that we forget how to get there! Here are a few steps that can help your brain find its flow:

First, set clear, specific goals that are realistic and achievable, as having specific goals is vital for getting to that state of flow. Having goals will give you direction and a sense of purpose, which in turn will keep you motivated and focused. As such, you should identify what you want to achieve, break it down into smaller tasks, and then create a timeline to track progress in order to hold yourself accountable.

Second, prioritize your tasks. Prioritizing tasks involves identifying the most critical tasks and completing them first. It will help you focus your energy and attention on what is most important and avoid distractions.

Third, eliminate distractions. Distractions can significantly deter getting into the state of flow. You should identify what distracts you the most and take steps to eliminate it in order to boost your flow and ultimately productivity. For example, turning off phone notifications, closing unnecessary computer tabs, or working in a quiet environment.

Fourth, set a timer. Identify how much time you have and set a timer so that you only work that amount of time. Setting a timer will help your brain reach flow faster, as it will improve your focus, assign a sense of urgency, and will eliminate the need to anticipate breaks. Because you know that when the timer is up, you get to take a break and do whatever you want.

On the other hand, you might not have goals identified yet, or your current goals don't align with what your brain truly enjoys. So, a good way to identify what you truly enjoy is to invest in what authors Bill Burnett and Dave Evans call a "Good Time Journal." A Good Time Journal offers a dedicated space for recording your experiences, both good and bad, and learning more about what truly makes you happy in life. You might start by setting aside some time before you go to sleep each night to reflect on how content or happy you were with your activities for the day. Likewise, jot down your feelings of boredom or discontentment. Eventually, this will help you identify the activities that put you in a state of flow.

Sleep and Exercise

It is no secret that good sleep and exercise are crucial for peak productivity. After all, one of the biggest keys to productivity and success is staying healthy. First, poor sleep is linked to productivity losses, which can cost employers close to $2,000 per employee per month.[10] Furthermore, getting enough sleep is vital for having good cognitive reaction times and accuracy.[11] So, it is of great importance that you try to get the recommended amount of sleep every night, which is at least seven hours for adults,[12] and if you can't get enough sleep one day, make sure you try to make it up on another. Not only does poor sleep hamper productivity, but it can also increase the risk of diabetes, heart disease, and stroke.[13] Hence, don't listen to all those productivity gurus that rave about sleeping less than six hours a day and working all the time. It is not healthy or sustainable, and evidence is stacked against that approach. So, focus on your health and get your sleep! However, getting enough sleep doesn't mean oversleeping in the morning, but rather prioritizing your sleep so you get to bed early in order to get the sleep that you need. After all, a lot of elite performers in various fields get up at 5 a.m. and dedicate at least the first hour of their day to being productive. That said, to follow what appears to be working for the many elite performers out there, you need to figure out how many hours of sleep your body truly needs. Figuring out how much sleep you need can easily be done by going to sleep when you have nothing the next day, not setting an alarm, and then calculating how much time you slept without being awakened by an external stimulus. Use that as a benchmark for how much sleep you truly need. Now, keep in mind that certain days would require more sleep based on your activity level the day before, so be flexible with yourself and try to accommodate your schedule to get or catch up on needed sleep as much as possible.

Exercise is another important factor that impacts productivity. First off, starting your day with a workout can be the best way to get your blood flowing and boost productivity, as only 10-15 minutes of moderate-intensity exercise can boost cognitive performance.[14] Moreover, exercise on work days can help boost your mood and increase your work performance.[15] One study showed that walking increased creativity by more than 80%![16] Hence, exercising for at least 10 minutes is vital for peak productivity; however, you should focus on low to moderate exercise rather than high-intensity exercise.[17]

Sleep and exercise are vital for productivity, but their benefit is only seen if they are done in a consistent matter!

Getting at least seven hours of sleep and at least 10 minutes of exercise is great for productivity only if they are done on a **regular basis**. As such, it is essential to habituate yourself to having these activities in your daily routine, which is a great segway to our next chapter about habit forming.

Habits

Habits are behaviors that we repeat with little conscious thought, so much so that they are performed automatically. Habits form through repetition and reinforcement, and they can have a significant impact on our lives. Habits can be good, like checking the rear-view mirror while driving or making sure the doors to your home are locked before you go to bed. Or they can be bad, like cigarette smoking. Once a habit is formed, it leaves a long-lasting impression that can alter the circuits of your brain.[18] That's why it is so hard to break a bad habit and hard to start a good one. It's pretty much like engraving in stone—hard to do and harder to erase.

Good habits are vital for success, as they are key for optimal productivity, concentration, memory, and creativity because when we wake up, we start our days with a finite amount of brain power. Hence, since habits are almost automatic actions done with minimal conscious thought, they don't consume any brain power, which will free the brain power available to be used in other activities and unleash your creativity. Even the most minute decisions that you make on a daily basis can add up and drain the precious limited brain power you have, and you can end up with what's called decision fatigue. That is why you see successful people like Mark Zuckerberg, Steve Jobs, and others seemingly wearing the same clothes all the time so they don't waste their available brain power on an irrelevant decision.

Habits generally form through repetition, reward, or discomfort relief. Nearly any habit that you can think of can be linked to one or all three of those triggers. First, a habit can be formed by repeating the action until it becomes second nature. Second, habits can form due to the reward received by certain actions. Third, habits can develop as a means to relieve discomfort. For instance, an example that encompasses all three is social media scrolling. In the beginning, we all just used to visit those sites, but then it became a habit through repetition, and now a day can't pass without visiting one of the social media sites. Social media can provide an instant reward in the form of a dopamine rush (dopamine is a brain neurotransmitter that is often associated with carrying signals of happiness and pleasure), and visiting those sites can provide relief from the greatest discomfort of all times, "boredom"! If you think you use social media too much or you are always on your phone, you are not alone. On average, people worldwide spend at least three hours on their phones every day, while almost half of all Americans spend at least four hours on their phones per day. Moreover, 50% of users will pick their phone up within three minutes of putting it down.[19] Certainly, this example shows the importance of getting our habits under control before they turn into addictions. What starts as an innocent action can turn into a bad habit that can put you off your goals. Fortunately, there are methods for developing good habits and breaking bad ones.

The first strategy is to make it obvious and easy. Let's say that you want to start a new habit of exercising first thing in the morning. So, how can you make it obvious and easy? Well, the first step is to make it obvious by specifying exactly what exercises you are going to do, for how many reps, and for how long. The second step is making it easy! So, don't plan to go the gym when you first start, rather exercise at home. Have your exercises ready to go the day before.

The second strategy is to start small and build gradually. Instead of trying to make a great change all at once, focus on making small, incremental changes. To go back to our previous example for exercising, you can start by doing pushups and sit-ups next to your bed for just five minutes every day after waking up and gradually increase the duration and intensity of your exercises over time.

The third strategy is that sometimes to build a new habit, you must break an existing one. But to break an existing one, whether it's bad or not, you need to define it and acknowledge its existence. For instance, let's say in our previous example that you are not able to start exercising first thing in the morning despite using the first couple of strategies. Then, you need to try to identify what habit is causing this and try to break it. Surely, staying up late every night won't help your efforts to start exercising first thing in the morning, as you will probably wake up tired every day, and that is ruining your chances of a new morning habit. After all, the desire for comfort and/or relief of discomfort is the root of all of our behavior. So, if you are tired, you are more likely to sleep in and not commit to your new early-morning exercise habit.

On the other hand, sometimes you can't break a habit without modifying its proximate habits. For instance, a friend of mine, "Jim," tried to quit smoking unsuccessfully for years until he actually stopped drinking coffee at the same time. Although it might seem weird at first, it actually makes perfect sense, as his smoking habit was closely linked in time and place to his coffee-drinking habit. He never drank coffee without a cigarette in his hand, so each time he resolved to quit smoking, he would break down once it was time to have his cup of Joe with his wife in the morning. By modifying the proximate habit of drinking coffee to only drinking tea (and not in the previous setting he was used to), he was able to quit smoking eventually.

The fourth strategy is to hold yourself accountable through documentation. Making or breaking a habit is just like any goal in life—it needs to be written down or your brain will find a way to dilute it or change it with time to something more comfortable! So, be conscious of your efforts and write down what you are planning on doing and keep it in a visible place. For instance, I will make such a note the wallpaper on my phone; that way, it is always on my mind, and my mind is always primed to take action toward my goal of breaking or adopting a new habit.

The fifth strategy is to always use positive statements to describe your habit goal. This behavior is especially important because, as humans, our brains are always attracted to the forbidden, so framing a goal in a negative statement might backfire. For example, if your goal is to develop a habit of always using the stairs at work, you should frame it as "I like to take the stairs at work, and I always want to take them," because if you frame it as "I won't take the elevator at work," your brain will trick you into thinking you're tired or your legs hurt. In short, your brain will find an excuse for you not to take the stairs and reverse the negative statement of "I won't take the elevator." At the end of the day, we all have had those moments when we had to pee, and the more we thought about not going to the bathroom, the more we wanted to go, so we would try to forget about it so the urge would go away. But the more you think that you don't want to go to the bathroom right now, the more you will end up wanting to go!

Having good habits, or what I like to call, good utilization of brain automation, is essential for success, health, and creativity, as they remove any effort required for your brain to do an action, and you will simply go through the motions of getting things done without stressing about every detail. It will free up more brain resources to think outside the box and make important decisions. Furthermore, brain automation for certain tasks will help bring about mastery in that field, as your brain will be focused on improvement rather than maintenance. On the other hand, when a habit is a bad one, it is difficult to break and requires more effort, as habits get engrained within our brains. Hence you should always be aware of what habits you are picking up and try to nip bad ones in the bud before they are fully engraved in your brain. Prevention is better than treatment. Nonetheless, if a bad habit is already there, the strategies presented earlier will ease the process of getting rid of it.

Anti-Procrastination Strategies

Procrastination is the act of deferring or postponing certain tasks, often to the point where they become urgent or even near impossible to complete. Furthermore, while procrastination is a relatively common issue, it can be the deciding factor of whether you will be successful in your endeavors or not. Thereby, it can have some serious consequences in terms of both your personal and your professional life. For instance, if you procrastinate doing a certain task at work, you risk missing a deadline, which will cause stress and anxiety that will negatively impact your mental health. Missing a deadline will lower your reliability at work and reflect badly on your career advancement going forward. Thus, it is important to have strategies to prevent and stop you from procrastinating. But, to overcome procrastination, it is necessary to first understand why we procrastinate. People procrastinate for four main reasons.

Four Main Reasons Behind Procrastination

Reason #1: Fear of Failure

Only the brave are successful in this life, but we need to distinguish between bravery and stupidity. You see, while some level of caution is important for preserving your well-being, excessive irrational fear of failure can have a negative impact on your personal and professional life. For example, last summer I went hiking with my family in the mountains of the Dead Sea, the lowest point on earth, and the trail was gorgeous! It took us through water trails, and we had to climb a steep hill, where we arrived at what our guide called the "fun part," which was a 30-foot-high cliff that we were supposed to jump from into a water reservoir. He led the way jumping and doing a back flip into the water; it was truly spectacular to see. Then came my turn, and I thought I was going to nail it, but as soon as I was on the edge of that cliff, I was crippled by fear. I mean, I couldn't move my legs an inch forward, nor was I close to actually jumping. The guide's aide tried to calm me down and give me a pep talk, but, no, my brain was not having it! You see, your brain's ultimate purpose is to preserve your well-being, so if it thinks you are not going to make it, it will try to stop you from jumping.

After a few failed attempts at takeoff, my brother pushed me! And I'm so glad he did because I ended up enjoying it so much that I kept climbing back up to do it again. As Henry Ford famously said, "One of the greatest discoveries a man makes, one of his great surprises, is to find he can do what he was afraid he couldn't do." Similarly, fear of failure can stop people from following their dreams, from starting their own business, or from getting into shape. Your mind will go into self-preservation mode, and it will start making failure the most likely outcome in order to preserve the status quo. Thankfully, there are steps we can take to overcome our fear of failure. First, start by identifying your fear. As with any issue, you have to know it so you can address it. Second, write it down in as much detail as you can. Third, write down a list of the worst-case scenarios that can happen; be creative and try to come up with as much as possible. Fourth, think of ways to prevent the worst-case scenarios from happening and solutions in the event they do happen. Fifth, scale back from the worst-case scenario to other things that can go wrong but are less significant until you get to the minute things that really don't matter if they happen or not. Try to come up with solutions for any significant issue that you can come up with, and if you can't come up with a solution, think of ways to prevent it from happening. Above all, remember to write everything down; whatever problem/solution you come up with, write it down. After all, what's not written is usually forgotten or sometimes altered by memory. This approach will help your brain think more logically about your situation, and you will be able to find out the best route for your goal. Even though all roads lead to Rome, not all of the roads are difficult to the same degree, so figuring this up will not only stop any irrational fear from manifesting, but it will also help you find the best route to take.

Reason #2: The Curse of Perfectionism

For me, perfectionism is the number one reason I procrastinate on exercise. I can't count how many times I said I'm not going to train today because I have already missed one day this week, so better to start fresh next week. And then comes next week, but another thing comes up, and so on. So, it is important to know that nothing is perfect! No time will be perfect, and no environment will be perfect. The perfect time to do anything is now! If you can't read 20 pages, read one. If you can't do 20 pushups, do one. As the Nike slogan goes, "Just do it."

Reason #3: Egotism

You might think to yourself, how can ego cause me to procrastinate? If you overestimate your abilities, you are bound to underestimate the resources and time needed for a task. For instance, when I was in college, a professor assigned us to write an article about the Seven Wonders of the World and the economic impact on countries where those wonders are located. He gave us a month to do the work. You can probably guess what I did. I knew I could do the article, so I kept postponing it until two days before the deadline when I started writing. Needless to say, I barely made it, and I got a B- on that. My ego got in my way, and I overestimated my knowledge of the subject and my ability to write, which ended up hurting my score. What I should have done instead, and what you should do, as well, if you experience similar feelings when handed a project, is to take it head-on. Sit down, write a project plan, determine the time to allow for each part to be done, and then assign a time each day to do the project tasks. Use a timer when you start each task. This way, you create a sense of urgency for each task, and you won't get blindsided by the iceberg of a project that you were only seeing the tip of.

Reason #4: Lack of Motivation

Motivation is the driving force that propels people to achieve their goals, aspirations, or desires. It is a complicated process involving both internal and external factors. For example, personal values, beliefs, and attitudes are examples of internal factors, whereas external factors include deficiency, rewards, and recognition. Motivation is the force needed for an action to happen. Therefore, lack of motivation is one of the most quoted reasons for procrastination. But in reality, that can be divided into two parts:

First, lack of motivation. Finding your true sense of purpose should be your ultimate goal in life, as it's at the core of anyone's internal happiness, satisfaction, and the driving force for getting things done. It is easy to get so carried away with all the distractions around us that you lose track of your internal spark. But how can you find your internal spark? Well, your first step would be to start a feel-good diary. Simply, at the end of your day, write down the aspects of your day that made you feel most alive and that gave you that electric feeling inside. Keep in mind that these insights don't have to be related to your job, and it is all about perspective. For instance, maybe it's spending time with your kids that gives you the most joy, and the income that you get from your job is what makes those moments happen. So, adjusting your perspective, in this case, will help you see that the point of the job is to have the time and ability to enjoy those moments with your kids. Or maybe, you find that you feel the spark when you are training a new employee, so you can start looking for an opportunity within your company to become a trainer, and if that's not a thing where you work, perhaps you can make it a thing. After all, sometimes you don't know something is needed until you try it. Changing your perspective about what you need to do by focusing on the end result will definitely help spark your motivation.

Second, what people sometimes mistakenly call "lack of motivation" is actually our brain prioritizing short-term pleasure and comfort over long-term goals. In other words, our brain is motivated to maintain the current state over the future state. So, basically, we would prefer to remain in our safe current state rather than risk it all for a future state that is not guaranteed. However, what we fail to acknowledge is that even our current state is not guaranteed to stay the same indefinitely. Needless to say, nothing ever stays the same. If you are not advancing, you are declining, but you just don't know it yet. For instance, think of the value of the "dollar": If you had

$1,000 in 1970 and chose to hide it in your mattress instead of investing it, it would be worth way less now because of inflation. So, we must always take action no matter how we feel! If the first step is a hard one, then break it down into baby steps and do that over and over until you get some traction. To put it in other words, think of it as if you are starting a fire—you don't start with the biggest log you can find, but rather, you start the fire with kindling. Then, once the fire starts, you start adding bigger and bigger logs. It's the same thing with motivation: If you are having trouble getting started, break it down into baby steps and keep doing that over and over until the fire inside of you is ignited and you can more easily take on bigger tasks.

One great way that helped me get started is author Mel Robbins's 5-Second Rule. It states that the moment you think about doing an activity, you have five seconds before your mind stops you from launching into it. She suggests that whenever that happens to you, count 5-4-3-2-1 and go as soon as you get to one—just like the countdown for a rocket. Once you hit go, you stop thinking and you start doing! On another note, the law of conservation of energy states that energy is neither created nor destroyed, and motivation is, at its base, a kind of energy. The small tasks will be the kindling that will get your inner fire going. As the saying goes, the journey of a thousand miles begins with a single step. And drop after drop, you can make an ocean.

Creativity

I never made one of my discoveries
through the process of rational thinking
Albert Einstein

C reativity is an essential human skill for success in all fields of life whether it is on a personal or a professional level. Creativity enables us to solve problems, express ourselves, and discover new opportunities. This chapter will look at the concept of creativity, its characteristics, and its significance. We will explore ways to develop and enhance your creativity. First, it is important to acknowledge that creativity can be learned and practiced. This has been shown in numerous studies, most notably a study by Reznikoff et al., where 117 pairs of twins were tested against 10 creativity tests to see whether or not genetics play a role in creativity. The experiment concluded that genetics doesn't play a major role in creativity,[20] hence creativity can be learned. In order to develop creativity, we must first understand it. According to the componential theory of creativity by Dr. Teresa Amabile, a Harvard Business School professor, creativity is influenced by four main factors.[21]

Four Main Factors of Creativity

Factor #1: Domain-related Skills

Knowledge in the field is essential. For instance, you wouldn't be able to become a musical composer without first knowing the musical keys, and you can't create the next big computer program without knowing how to code. We always need a strong foundation in order to support our creative endeavors. But here, it is essential to point out that knowledge in the field doesn't mean knowing the rules so you can adhere strictly to them, as that will ultimately hinder creativity. In other words, don't let the preconceived notions of a field constrain your train of thought. As Pablo Picasso once said, "Learn the rules like a pro, so you can break them like an artist."

Factor #2: Process-related Skills

This relates to how you approach problems and come up with solutions. For example, let's say I asked you how to find the parameter of a square that has a 4 cm side. You can say all sides are the same length, so the parameter would be 4 + 4 + 4 + 4 = 16, or you can say the equation for finding the parameter of a square is 4 x a side so it will be 4 x 4 = 16, or you can use a ruler and measure it out. All methods will yield the same answer although they resemble different thought paths based on preconceived knowledge and ways of thinking.

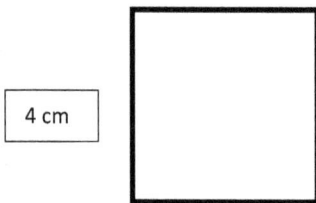

Factor #3: Motivation

This represents the passion to solve a problem for the mere joy of working on it, which was discussed in greater detail in the previous chapter. For instance, to help drive the point through, as unusual as it is, when I was a kid, I used to get a great amount of satisfaction solving math problems. There was something about figuring out a solution to a problem that brought me a great amount of mental joy.

Factor #4: Social environment

This refers to where you live or work. Our environment plays an important role in stimulating or hindering our creativity. The proverb goes, "Tell me who your friends are, and I will tell you who you are" because your friends are an aspect of your environment that can affect your attitudes, goals, and perspectives. So, if you want greatness, you have to surround yourself with great people, which is why having a mentor is effective, as we discussed earlier in this book. On the other hand, if your place of business or home is not supportive of your ideas, that will definitely hamper your creativity. If your mind gets used to having your ideas shut down, it will stop exploring new ideas as a means to protect your feelings and avoid rejection.

Now that we have discussed factors that influence creativity, let's talk about techniques to find our creative edge and boost our creative thinking skills.

Techniques to Boost Creative Thinking Skills

Inversion

If you have ever watched the TV show *Seinfeld*, you are probably familiar with the episode called "The Opposite," where George Costanza decides to toss his gut instincts to the curb and do the opposite of what he usually does, and it works out great for him! That episode is not just a comedic masterpiece, but it also highlights an important principle that can help boost creativity, which is the principle of inversion, in which you play out a scenario in your head wherein you do the opposite of what you would usually do and see where that takes you. This will break your brain's usual train of thought and force it to take new scenarios into consideration, which will ultimately improve your creativity.

Familiarity and Repetition

In order to be creative in a certain field, you need to have knowledge of the field (domain-related as mentioned previously), and this, coupled with repetition of certain tasks, will result in your mind automating these tasks to free it for creativity and innovation. According to psychologist Mihaly Csikszentmihalyi, founder of Flow Theory, before any innovation happens, people must go through a number of steps that lead to creativity and insight. To put it another way, ideas can only arise from a solid foundation of knowledge and preparation.[22] Correspondingly, there appears to be a number of hours required to reach the point at which frustration with a task produces creative insight into new ways of doing that task.[23] Although it was suggested by author Malcolm Gladwell in his book *Outliers* that you need an average of 10,000 hours of deliberate practice to become an expert and achieve greatness in a field, this number is definitely not set in stone, and it will differ from person to person depending on a variety of factors including the quality of practice, your ability to learn, and so on. But one thing for certain is that your experience in the field and repetition are needed to inspire creativity in a field.

Open Mind

In order to unleash our creativity, we should train our brains to stay open-minded and assess all ideas carefully rather than jumping to judgment. Simply put, you need to suspend your ego and approach any idea with what I call an "idiot-wanting-to-learn mentality." Having this mentality will suspend your ego, and it will help your mind break out of its preconceived notions. Moreover, you should approach any thought or opinion you hear with a questioning mindset, even if it's from a so-called expert. Interestingly, psychologist and political scientist Philip Tetlock found that there an inverse relationship between the reputation of an expert and their respective accuracy; in other words, the more media appearances the expert has, the more likely they are wrong.[24] It is of vital importance to have an open mind with a questioning attitude so you don't let the false opinions of others shape your way of thinking. It is easy to think that we have the best perspective on a matter, but that's only because it's the only one we know. So, train yourself to put your ego aside and have a skeptical, open mind that can help you set your creativity free.

Begin with the End in Mind

You might ask yourself, "How can I start with the end in mind when I'm trying to be creative and find something new?" Well, you can do that by forecasting what you envision your end product to be and using that as a reference point upon which you build a structured way of thinking. In short, structure can help shape creative pursuits. So, instead of starting from scratch, begin with the end in mind, then give it some structure and creativity will follow.

Multidisciplinary Knowledge

If you want to be creative and innovative in one field, you need to be a polymath rather than a specialist in that field. Don't get me wrong, having specialized knowledge is essential for creativity, as we discussed earlier in the "familiarity and repletion" section. However, you shouldn't limit your knowledge to that specific field; instead, you should develop scientific curiosity and broaden your knowledge to other fields. In other words, be a specialist in one or two fields and a generalist in other fields, as that will increase your chances of greatness. Michigan State University Professor Robert Bernstein's research shows that Nobel Prize-winning scientists were more likely to have multidisciplinary knowledge rather than specialized knowledge. Furthermore, they were more likely to engage in other creative outlets like music, dancing, or performing.[25] Hence, if you want to be creative, you'll need to be explorative, develop a scientific curiosity in multiple fields, and not be restricted by specialty skills. For instance, Nikola Tesla was a theoretical and experimental physicist, mathematician, electrical engineer, mechanical engineer, and inventor. There are numerous examples throughout history of famous polymaths; to name a few: Aristotle, Al-Khwarizmi, Ibn Sina, Leonardo Da Vinci, Benjamin Franklin, and many others.

Attitude

Your attitude towards life is a great predictor of your success. Studies have shown that being positive can boost your creativity and problem-solving skills.[26] For instance, one study found that induction of positive emotions among physicians can boost their creativity in solving problems and result in greater job satisfaction,[27] whereas another study showed that you can boost creative ingenuity in participants by having them watch a short comedy film or by giving them a small bag of candy.[28] Hence, harnessing a positive attitude is vital for the creative mind. So, how can we develop and maintain a positive attitude?

Embrace failure: Our exam-based school systems have trained our minds to avoid failure at all costs and have framed it as the absolute worst thing that can happen to us. However, having this mentality is dangerous for the creative mind, as it focuses on avoiding failure rather than thinking outside of the box. As Edwin Catmull, author of *Creativity, Inc.,* cofounder of Pixar Animation, and at one point, the president of Walt Disney and Pixar Animation Studios puts it, "If you aren't experiencing failure, then you are making a far worse mistake: You are being driven by the desire to avoid it." Failure is a rite of passage for successful people, but you should be learning from each failure and documenting it well, as those who don't learn from their mistakes are bound to repeat them, which reminds me of a famous quote by Thomas Edison after he invented the light bulb. It took him more than 1,000 attempts to find the right material to make the light bulb, and he famously said, "I have not failed 10,000 times. I have not failed once. I have succeeded in proving that those 10,000 ways will not work. When I have eliminated the ways that will not work, I will find the way that will work." So, don't fear failure, but embrace it, learn from it, and most importantly, don't focus on avoiding it, as only then can you unshackle your creative mind.

Be curious: When it comes to creativity, the more curious you are, the better! A curious mind is a questioning mind, and that is a great stimulant of creativity. Furthermore, being curious means that you value learning above anything else, and that has a way of freeing your mind from self-imposed deadlines that can sequester your creativity. Curiosity can improve our mental and physical energy, result in superior performance, and is associated with higher intelligence.[29] Additionally, intentionally inducing your curiosity can boost your creativity and enhance your memory.[30] A great way to enhance your curiosity is to approach everything with a questioning mindset. In other words, have a dialog with yourself and ask yourself open-ended questions: Why does that happen? What if...? How can it happen? And, don't be afraid of your answers appearing silly, as that might still lead to new discoveries. After all, what's silly today can be a mind-boggling reality in the future. Flying was considered a silly notion at some point in time, and now it is a reality.

Daydreaming: Daydreaming or mind-wandering is the process of participating in an internal stream of thinking that is unconnected to the present moment. Daydreaming has been shown to enhance creative thinking. Nonetheless, not all daydreaming is associated with the same effect, as was shown by a recent study that found that only two types of daydreaming are associated with increased creativity. The two types of daydreams associated with enhanced creativity are those that are personally meaningful and those with fantastical content.[31] In general, studies have shown that people think more creatively when they give themselves breaks and engage in daydreaming.[32] So, don't feel like you're being lazy if you take some time to daydream, as that might be key to boosting your creativity. But don't take this as an excuse to procrastinate either. Rather, you should set a timer for, say, ten minutes where you purposefully daydream and document your daydreams after each session.

Physical activity: Studies have shown that an increase in physical activity is associated with enhanced creativity.[33] One study where participants were asked to go through some creativity tests both while walking and sitting down found that walking was associated with around a 60% increase in creativity.[34] Furthermore, walking outdoors in the same study boosted creativity more than walking indoors on a treadmill. The fluidity of the movement may play a role in the enhancement of creativity, as well. Most notable was another study in which participants were asked to move their arms loosely and fluidly through space, tracing the lines of a looping and curvy line-drawing to simulate dancing, while another group traced a straighter, more angular drawing. It was found that participants who moved their arms as if they were dancing had better creative thinking and original thoughts.[35] So, in order to be more creative, think about taking a 10-minute walk, preferably outside, or turning on some good music and dancing to the rhythm for a few minutes.

On another note, having good nighttime sleep habits appears to be as vitally important as physical activity for optimal creativity. Multiple studies have shown that a good night's sleep can boost creative thinking.[36] One study showed that creativity can be enhanced by using a priming technique to stimulate problem-solving while sleeping. Simply smelling a scent while thinking about the problem before sleeping and then having a diffuser release the same smell after you have fallen asleep was shown to enhance creativity.[37] Hence, whether it is a regular good night's sleep or sleep primed by a certain smell, research supports the creativity-enhancing effect of a good night's sleep!

Memory

L et's start this chapter with a short story about a man, who in 1953 at the age of 27 years old, underwent brain surgery in an attempt to cure his epileptic seizures. During the procedure, the neurosurgeon removed his entire hippocampus, and although the operation was successful in reducing the frequency of his seizures, it left him in a state of global memory loss in which he lost 11 years' worth of memories from the period before surgery and also lost the ability to form new memories. His experience went on to become the most studied medical case in history, with nearly 12,000 mentions of his name in journal articles.[38] This story resonates with me, as I have played out being in that scenario multiple times in my mind. Imagining going through what he went through at 27 years old made me think more about the importance of what we take for granted every day, from how we cherish our fondest memories, to how we do our jobs, to how we find our way home, and to how we know our own names. Our memories are an essential part of our existence. Not only do they signify time for us, but without them, there is no yesterday or tomorrow; there is only today. Furthermore, it is extremely difficult to have any sort of profession if you can't remember the basics in your field and can't continue to learn new things in your field. Having a great memory is a valuable trait for success. So, how can we preserve and improve our memories?

The Brain Is a Muscle

First, it is important to think of our memory, and our brain in general, as a muscle that becomes better with training. Similar to physical exercise, unless you have the discipline to regularly train your memory and continuously improve it through adopting new techniques and practicing them, you won't see any real improvement. Hence, the first step to improving your memory is to train it on a regular schedule! Just like the other muscles in my body, where I have a day to do legs and a day to do chest exercises and so on, I have a day every week where I exercise my memory by trying to memorize information or book pages. Interestingly, a highly publicized study of

London taxi drivers, who were required to memorize all the routes of London (nearly 25,000 city streets), found that their posterior hippocampi were significantly larger than those of people who didn't drive a taxi.[39] In lay terms, this shows our mind's elasticity and signifies our mind's ability to restructure to accommodate our memorization needs.

Hence, I use mind games and puzzles to exercise my brain for 5-10 minutes each day. I use an app called Elevate for this purpose (Disclaimer: I'm not sponsored by or have any financial connections to this app; I just like it.) There is data from numerous studies that show that training your brain, and more specifically your memory, can slow cognitive decline in Alzheimer's disease.[40] For instance, one trial that was supported by the U.S. National Institute on Aging and the U.S. National Institute for Nursing Research randomly assigned more than 2,800 healthy people with a mean age of 74 to one of four groups: memory training, reasoning training, speed training, and a "no contact" control group that was used to see what the effects of repeated testing would be. Participants in each of the training groups received 10 sessions of training. Interestingly, those who received one of the three training regimens continued to perform significantly better five years later than people who received no training.[41] In another study, cognitively active people were more than two times less likely to develop Alzheimer's disease.[42] So, although it may sound trivial, playing some mind games and exercises might help boost your memory capabilities and potentially lower your risk of developing AD.

Memorization Improvement Tips

Presence and understanding: Be fully engaged in what you are trying to memorize. Read with the purpose of explaining a topic to someone. For instance, whenever I'm trying to memorize something new, I first read it while visualizing myself explaining it to someone else. This helps my brain think of it as a memory rather than a task. Furthermore, you should focus on immersing yourself in the experience rather than using technology to capture it. Indeed, a study looking into whether photographing objects affects what people remember about them found that participants taking a tour in a museum who observed objects without taking pictures of them remembered far more details than participants who took pictures of the objects.[43] On another note, being present is vital to avoid those embarrassing moments when you meet someone new and immediately forget their name! We all have been through those moments, and I have been on the other end of a lot of those encounters, but those can easily be avoided through being present and using what I call the RAU technique, which stands for Repeat, Ask, and Use. First, repeat the person's name to them to make sure you heard it correctly. Second, ask about the spelling of the name and its meaning or origins. Third, use their name while talking to them.

Time of day: Generally speaking, time of day can affect the ease of which you can memorize a subject. For instance, from experience, the best time to memorize is "Fajr" time, which is any time between dawn and sunrise. This is further supported by research, which shows that students who are early birds achieve higher GPAs than their night owl counterparts.[44] To find Fajr time in your area, Google sunrise and dawn time, and Fajr time would be the time between those two. Its duration will differ depending on your geographical location, but usually, it will be around one hour or more.

Visualize: Your imagination is your best friend when it comes to solid memorization, and associating more out-of-the-ordinary images with what you are trying to memorize is the best practice, as our minds are wired to detect the unusual and disregard the usual. Furthermore, your imagination can be used to boost your memorization skill by using the loci technique, or what's sometimes referred to as "Memory Palace," which is featured in numerous books like *Unlimited Memory* by Kevin Horsley and *Memory Palace* by Lewis Smile. The loci technique is a strategy for remembering information that involves placing a mental picture for each thing to be recalled at a different location along an imaginary journey. The information may then be recalled in the correct sequence by mentally retracing the same path through the imaginary journey and turning the mental pictures back into the facts that they represent. To use this technique, you first need to create your locations, which should be places that you are familiar with and already engraved in your memory, like the home you grew up in or the surroundings on your way to work. Second, make a list of things that you want to memorize, and imagine each item in one location of your prespecified locations, making this your memory palace.

Take notes: Handwritten notes using pen and paper enhance your ability to retain information. It is important to stress the "handwritten on pen and paper" part, as handwriting notes using pen and paper was proven, in a study conducted by the University of Tokyo,[45] to be far superior to any electronic means of note-taking, even notes handwritten on an iPad.

Laughter! It helps to associate what you are trying to learn with humor. A survey conducted by Pew Research Center showed that viewers of comedy news shows, like *The Daily Show* and *The Colbert Report,* exhibited higher retention of news facts than any other news media sources like network news programs and major newspapers.[46] Moreover, appropriate, topic-related humor by an instructor is effective in improving students' retention of information.[47]

Learning

Learning is a process of acquiring knowledge and skills through experience, study, and instruction. In this chapter, we will explore techniques to boost your learning ability. First, it is essential to know your personal learning style. With more than 70 known, different learning styles, knowing your learning style is vital for you to optimize your approach to learning. Notably, the four most common types of learning styles are visual, aural, verbal (reading/writing), and kinesthetic (VARK). For this purpose, there are online questionnaires that can help you figure out your learning style if you don't already know it. You can also identify your learning style on your own by understanding what each learning style represents. First, visual learners understand information better when it's presented in a visual way, for example through pictures, diagrams, and written instructions, whereas aural learners learn better when a topic is presented through sound. They would prefer to listen to a lecture on a subject rather than read a book about it. Next, verbal learners learn better through writing and reading. And last but not least are kinesthetic learners, who tend to learn through doing and experiencing things. Most of us use a mix of learning styles when learning, and certain learning styles are better suited for different subjects. For instance, a welder learns more by doing rather than by reading a book on welding. Hence, if you are having trouble learning a subject, you can try to overcome it by modifying the topic presentation to suit your learning style. If you want to learn about stock trading, say, but you can't understand the topic through books, you might want to try and find lectures about it or an audiobook on the subject. Similarly, if you can't grasp a subject by listening to a lecture, you can search for a book on the topic, and so on.

Knowing your preferred learning style will help you optimize your learning experience, but there are additional techniques to help you learn more in a shorter time.

Pre-Reviewing

Pre-reviewing can help you get enough background information and highlights to help you read through a topic faster and better understand it. For instance, Formula 1 drivers spend significant amounts of time getting to know the racetrack through test labs, simulators, and maps of the track to enable them to achieve the fastest times possible on race day. Similarly, pre-reviewing a topic or a book will prime your brain to focus on the main points of the topic while speeding through the filler.

Speed-Reading

Speed-reading is a different approach to reading that is more guided and focused, resulting in a faster reading speed. Although this skill is a great one to have, especially in our day and age with an abundance of great books and articles being published, it is worth noting that despite the popular notion that speed reading doesn't affect comprehension, research studies have shown that it does actually affect comprehension. Specifically, speed reading seems to affect high comprehension, hence it can be used whenever reading the text with moderate comprehension is acceptable.[48] With that said, let's dive into techniques to help improve your reading speed:

Indenting: This can help improve your reading speed, as your mind focuses on the middle chunk of a sentence. First, you should start by previewing the text and identifying the main talking points and keywords. This works by training your brain to focus your gaze on the middle portion of a sentence, about half an inch to an inch from the beginning and end of each sentence. This will help you increase your reading speed, as your brain can make out the entire line by only the middle section.

Using a pacer: Using your finger or a pen as a pacer to guide your eyes will force your eyes into moving in the direction of the pacer, thereby increasing your reading speed.

Subvocalization: Subvocalization is the process of speaking to oneself silently while reading. Although this may aid understanding, as you can hear the words along with seeing them, it can interfere with your reading speed, as then you can only read as fast as you can say the words. So, getting rid of subvocalization can significantly increase your reading speed, and this can be done by humming a song, chewing gum, or counting 1-2-3 while you are reading. Basically, you're trying to engage your voice with something else so it won't interfere with your reading speed.

Vocabulary knowledge: Having a large vocabulary is the most significant factor that affects your reading speed. That this, coupled with practice, is the only way to effectively increase your reading speed without jeopardizing high comprehension was shown by Professor Keith

Rayner et al. in a comprehensive review article published in the *Journal of Psychological Science in the Public Interest* in 2016 .[49]

Regression: Regression, or backtracking, is the process of re-reading part of the text. For instance, you finish reading a page in a book and you go back to read it again. Interestingly, it has been reported that an average reader will spend around 20 minutes of every hour re-reading the material.[50] In general, regression happens naturally to improve comprehension, eliminate apparent contradictions in comprehension, or improve visual word recognition.[51] However, it can become more of a habitual behavior unrelated to comprehension. Hence, it is important to be conscious of your regression and use methods such as reading with purpose, using a pacer, or the 50/50 rule (or an adaptation of it). The 50/50 rule, as presented by author Thomas Oppong, states that you should spend 50% of your allotted time for reading and the other 50% for explaining the material to someone else. Using the principle of this rule, you should adapt the idea to different percentages as it suits you. For example, I can explain what I read in 30 minutes to another person in less than 10 minutes. As such, I read with the purpose of using 30% of the allotted time to talk about what I have read to someone else (i.e., my wife).

Meta-Learning

Meta-learning can be thought of as the ability to consciously guide your own learning journey, and it consists of two main parts: metacognition, which is the process of learning about learning, and having a growth mindset, which is the belief that one's abilities can be improved through hard work. In fact, some of the following techniques in this chapter would fall under this concept.

Mind Mapping

Mind-mapping is a non-linear learning strategy that helps learners analyze and explore topics by employing visual-spatial links. Several studies have shown the importance of mind maps in enhancing learning, comprehension, and critical thinking skills in students.[52] For instance, a research study done on business students attending a class for E-business, where students were assigned to two different groups, the first to learn the topic the conventional way and the second to learn the topic through mind maps, found that students who used mind maps were more motivated to learn and were able to establish better connections between theoretical and empirical knowledge.[53] Similarly, in another study done on English as a second language students, the use of mind maps was found to improve students' reading comprehension.[54] Furthermore, by breaking down a topic into smaller portions, it becomes easier to memorize and understand. So, how do we go about creating a mind map for a topic? First of all, mind maps are basically a method of visually organizing information in a spider diagram. To start, you need to pinpoint the central concept of the topic. Then, major ideas related to this topic are connected to it, and ideas connected to those ideas branch out of them, and so on, as in the following example of a simple mind map of the nervous system:

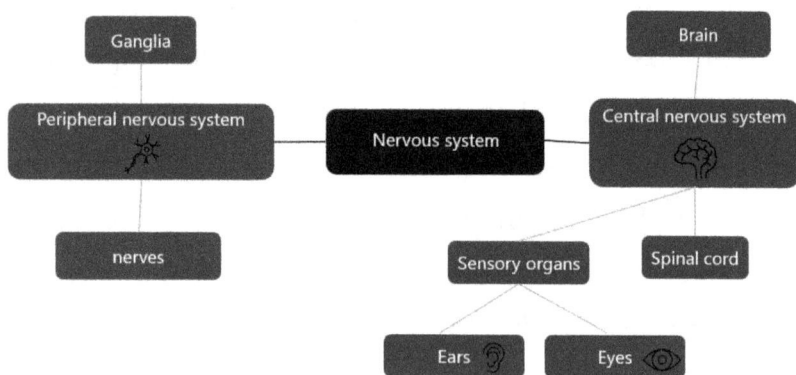

Reflection and Feedback

Soliciting feedback and self-reflection is an effective method for learning and personal development. Specifically, this is of great importance to ensure that you are on track with your learning goal through feedback from your peers, friends, family, and most importantly, from your own reflection on how you are doing. Feedback and reflection can help you identify areas of growth, thereby making you a better learner. So, always accept feedback with an open mind and remember that no matter how much you know, there is someone who knows more! As the Chinese proverb goes, "Empty your cup."

Spaced Repetition

Spaced repetition is using short study periods spread over long periods of time rather than trying to study everything in a long, tedious study session. Numerous studies have shown that dividing your study sessions into small study sessions rather than cramming everything into one long session is far superior in terms of better memorization and problem-solving.[55] For instance, a study done on sixth graders studying a map of Latin America found that students who were assigned to a spaced repetition program of learning achieved better results than those who didn't use spaced repetition.[56] One way to incorporate this into your learning schedule is to try to recall what you memorized and studied 24 hours after you have learned it, and if you recall it perfectly, then do it again after another 24 hours, and so on. Or, you can attempt to increase the interval between tests so that the next time you repeat the information is at 36 hours, and the next is at 48 hours, and so on, similar to the Leitner System. However, it should be noted that there is currently no strong evidence supporting the notion that one particular time interval between sessions is superior (whether it is increasing the time interval, keeping it the same, or even decreasing it), but increasing the number of times you repeat the information over a spaced interval is associated with up to a 200% increase in long-term recall over repetition without any spacing.[57] To sum up this idea, using spaced repetition for memorizing and learning material is an effective method for faster and better memorization.

Free Recall

Free recall will help you better organize your knowledge and facilitate your learning of future and past material. Simply put, free recall is the act of writing down from memory everything you learned once you have finished reading or studying it. Not only does free recall enhance your learning and memorization of material, but it also strongly improves subsequent learning and memorization of unrelated material, acting as a "potent memory enhancer."[58] To practice, at the end of your reading of this book for today, stop and write down everything that you remember you learned about. This will improve your memorization of what you have read, and it will stimulate your ability to memorize and learn future material. Better yet, rather than just writing down everything that you remember from the material in a note format only, write it down in a question-and-answer format, as that was shown to be superior to regular note-taking in the long run.[59] For instance, if I was reading the previous paragraph for the first time now and wanted to apply the concept of "free recall," then as soon as I'm done reading it, I will write down on a separate piece of paper what I remember, which could be " the act of writing down what I remember about a subject after finishing learning about it," and I will write before it or next to it, "What is free recall?" This method combines testing with note-taking and will likely provide better learning than either method alone.

Deliberate Practice

Deliberate practice is a systematic and goal-oriented type of practice, which involves focus and practicing for the sole purpose of enhancing performance. Moreover, it should be noted that regular practice and experience are not the same as deliberate practice, as the latter is a method of skill development that involves setting objectives, breaking down work, obtaining feedback, and sustaining strong attention. It takes perseverance, patience, and dedication to ongoing growth. This concept was first conceptualized by Anders Ericsson and his colleagues in the early 1990s, and since then, this concept has been presented in numerous books and publications highlighting its effectiveness and value. In fact, if 10% of a skill is due to talent, the other 90% will be due to deliberate practice. In other words, you don't have to be talented in a field to be great at it; it sure doesn't hurt, but the actual proponent of greatness is deliberate practice.

Take the case of László Polgár, the Hungarian psychologist who believed geniuses are made, not born. Polgar and his wife got married to conduct an experiment in which they were going to teach their kids a particular subject and have them specialize in that particular topic with continuous deliberate practice from a young age, as young as four years old for the eldest child. The topic the Polgárs decided to experiment with was chess, and their experiment was successful, with all of their three daughters becoming chess prodigies and one of them becoming the most successful female chess champion ever. Hence, although innate talent has a role in being successful in a field, deliberate practice has a more significant impact on success, regardless of the presence of innate talent. To elaborate, think of your skill as a fruit tree seed, and your seed is either already planted (innate talent), or you are planting it with your interest and curiosity. Having a seed already pre-planted will help, but unless you take care of it (deliberate practice), it will remain a seed in the dirt and will never become a fruit tree. So, how do we go about applying deliberate practice to develop expert-level performance and knowledge in a field? And how much deliberate practice is needed to achieve greatness in a field?

First, deliberate practice requires that you break down complex topics or skills for which you want to develop expert-level knowledge/performance into smaller, more manageable parts and that you work on those parts one by one. Furthermore, you should write down all the parts and create a clear plan that shows the sequence of parts and the planned timeline to go through them. Next, prior to starting a study or training session in a part, you need to set clear goals that you intend to reach by going through this training session. Moreover, those goals should be measurable and attainable within the timeframe of each session.

Second, deliberate practice requires the presence of immediate and informative feedback, which can come from a variety of sources, including your instructors, coaches, peers, and your own self-evaluation. By soliciting feedback, you will be better able to identify your weaknesses and correct errors, thereby refining your training technique and refocusing your efforts on the areas of practice that most need it. Deliberate practice is a continuous improvement process in which you keep raising your standards for acceptable performance with the help of feedback as you progress further.

Lastly, the amount of deliberate practice needed to attain expert-level skills and knowledge is somewhat impacted by interpersonal differences; however, studies have shown that a minimum of 3,000 hours of deliberate practice is needed to achieve mastery.[60]

Summary of steps to apply deliberate practice:

1. Define the goal of your study/training.

2. Break down the project into smaller, more manageable parts.

3. Write down a plan with a defined sequence of parts.

4. Determine a measurable, attainable goal for each training session.

5. Continuously solicit feedback from your peers, teachers, or self-assessment (remember free recall, and test yourself at regular intervals).

6. Continuously refine your training strategy and speed based on received feedback.

Communication Skills

G reat communication skills are vital for success in all areas of life. Having effective communication skills will enable you to convey your thoughts effectively, thereby improving your chances of success and building strong relationships. No matter how much knowledge and experience you have in a field, you are never going to be successful without the proper communication skills. You can be the smartest person in the room, but that means nothing if you can't express your smart ideas to other people. Also, you are a social being, and the way you communicate your thoughts and emotions might be the difference between having a great social life surrounded by a circle of close friends and family or going through life alone. As Ali Ibn Abi Talib once said, "You are master of what you say until you utter it; once you deliver it, you are its captive. Preserve your tongue as you do your gold and money. One word could bring disgrace and the termination of a bliss." I would go as far as to say that knowing how to communicate effectively with people is the single most important skill anyone can have!

In general, good communication depends on the following factors:

The What?

The content of what you are saying is a crucial aspect of communication mastery, as it forms the foundation of what is being conveyed from information and ideas. Furthermore, it is the essence of establishing meaningful connections between individuals. Whether it's a professional discussion, an important negotiation, or a casual conversation, the substance of our words holds the ultimate power to inform, influence, connect, and inspire others. In other words, the quality of the conversation and/or speech is ultimately dependent on the value added from your content. Nonetheless, some factors can affect the quality of what you are saying:

Honesty

First of all, honesty is the basis of all true connections; however, being honest doesn't mean it is okay to be disrespectful! Instead, you should find the right words to convey your truth. For instance, if you run a company and one of your employees has missed the mark on one of his projects, you can tell him that he did a horrible job, which would be the honest truth, but it would ultimately create resentment between the two of you. Instead, by choosing other words to convey your truth, you could say, "I know you could have done better on this project, and I want to help you get there by trying to figure out where we might have gone wrong."

"I Want to Help" Attitude

Second, you should approach your conversations and presentations with an "I want to help" attitude and not a "how can I benefit from this" attitude. This will leave you more attentive and open to conversation. Furthermore, it will significantly lower your stress levels, as it is always harder to ask for something than to give it. As Winston Churchill said, "We make a living by what we get, but we make a life by what we give."

This Is a Conversation

Third, it is important to go into any conversation or speech with the goal of the conversation in mind. This is of vital importance, especially when you are talking about difficult conversations at home or work, as sometimes you might get into an argument with your partner about something, and it can grow into something else, and your goal when you started the conversation gets lost in the who-is-right and who-is-wrong, which is meaningless! So many people lose contact with friends and family members over a stupid argument, and no one remembers why it started in the first place. So, it becomes arguing for the sake of arguing, which is never productive. However, if you go into a conversation with a specific, defined goal, you are more likely to get a result out of it.

On another note, you should be cognizant of the power of the framing effect and the prospect theory (sometimes referred to as the Loss-Aversion Theory) as developed by psychologists Daniel Kahneman and Amos Tversky.[61] Simply put, people are more affected by the probability of loss than by the similar probability of gain; moreover, they tend to value certainty over risk, especially when gains and losses are equal in likelihood. For example, let's say you are playing a game and behind door number 1 there is $500, whereas behind door number 2 there is a 50% chance of winning $3,000. Which one will you choose? According to this theory, you are more likely to choose door number 1, as there is a guaranteed $500, so you avoid the potential loss involved in choosing door number 2. However, were the situation reframed, you could be induced to select door number 2. Let's change the game to one in which the top prize is $3,000, and all you had to do is pick the right door. Now, with door number 1, you lose 83% of the top prize instantly, but with door number 2, you have a 50% greater chance of winning the $3,000 than with door number 1. In this context, you will be more likely to choose door number 2, as this option was framed in a more positive light. Hence, by creating the right context for your discussion, negotiation, or conversation, you can get the reaction you are looking for from your listeners.

The How?

The second factor after "content" that has a great impact on the quality of your communication is the quality of your voice. The quality of your communication depends on your clarity, tone and pitch, volume, and pace.

Clarity

First of all, clarity. Information delivered by people using clear speech is generally better understood. To speak clearly means that you should be pronouncing and enouncing each word and sentence correctly. Whereas pronunciation refers to the sound each word makes when spoken aloud, enunciation refers to stating each word completely and distinctly. This plays a bigger role when you have a different accent or dialect than your listeners. Because different accents can influence how others understand you and similar words can mean different things based on the dialect, you should make an effort to pronounce words clearly. You should also acknowledge your accent and provide a safe space for your listener to question the intended meaning of your words. As a person who grew up outside of the U.S., I'm always aware of my accent, and I check with my listeners if I notice that look of misunderstanding on their faces. So, whenever I feel that whomever I'm talking to is confused by what I've said, I simply smile and say, "I'm sorry, I might have lost you with my accent, so I just want to check if we are on the same page." Although you should always be aware of your accent to promote better understanding, you should never be ashamed of having an accent! Having an accent is part of what makes you unique, and it is nothing to be ashamed of; however, it shouldn't be an excuse for poor communication.

Different dialects within a country or a region are also something to be aware of, as they affect understanding. An example that I always like to use in the U.S.—even though it might not rise to a matter of "dialect" per se, it does help drive the point home—is "pop" vs. "soda" vs. "coke." Although they all refer to the same thing (a soft drink), "pop" is the term used in the Midwest and West; whereas "soda" is more likely to be heard in the Northeast, Florida, and California; and most everywhere in the South you hear it referred to as "coke," whether it's actually made by the Coca-Cola Company or not. As simple as it is, in order to communicate effectively with a restaurant server, you have to be aware of the differences in dialects.

Additionally, when trying to speak clearly, you should focus on keywords related to your subject, as that will help maintain your listeners' attention. Lastly, a proper breathing technique is essential for speaking clearly, as a strong, confident voice can command attention and convey authority, whereas a hesitant or timid voice may not be as persuasive. Hence, a proper breathing technique is essential to enhancing your communication effectiveness.

Surely, the best place to go to observe optimal breathing techniques, especially as it relates to a public speaking setting, is the opera, as opera singers possess incredible breathing techniques to help them sing with a full and rich voice. Former opera singer and bestselling author Allison Shapira gives an example of such a technique in her 2015 article in *Harvard Business Review* in which she shows how you can utilize the power of deep breathing to enhance your communication effectiveness. I recommend reading the article so you can get the full essence of the technique—I will leave the link in the references section of this book, or you can simply google it.[62]

Vocal Attributes

Second, your vocal attributes, such as the tone, pitch, pace, rhythm, and volume of your voice, can help you convey your emotions, intentions, and attitudes. We are emotional beings, so adjusting the tone or pitch of what is being said can drastically change what is understood. For instance, you can say "I feel excited," but if your tone doesn't reflect the excitement that you are feeling, it will be perceived by your listener as a sarcastic comment or that you are lying. The pitch and tone of your voice can help express excitement, empathy, concern, or other emotions and should match the words being said for effective communication. On another note, the volume in which you speak plays a role, as well. For instance, speaking too softly may make it difficult for others to hear you and might convey a picture of shyness or embarrassment to your listeners, while speaking too loudly might be overwhelming to your listeners and be mistaken for rudeness or anger.

Moreover, the speed at which you speak is of vital importance, as speaking too quickly can make it challenging for your listeners to understand you, while speaking too slowly may lead your listeners to boredom or frustration. Lack of variation in any of those vocal attributes can lead to a monotonous style of communication that will act as a sleeping aid to your listeners, and people will quickly lose interest in listening to you. Instead, you should express your emotions in your speech by varying your vocal attributes to emphasize your point. For instance, you can change your tone and speak louder to show the importance of a main point. It goes without saying that effective communication requires the utilization of the sound power in your voice by altering tone, pitch, and pace, and by raising or lowering your voice based on the points you want to stress in a discussion or presentation.

Body Language

Third, your body language is an integral element of effective communication. It facilitates the expression of emotions, interests, and attitudes, and it reinforces verbal messages. Positive body language includes smiling, nodding, leaning forward, maintaining eye contact, and relaxing your body posture and position. Research shows that maintaining an open body position will reflect more positively on how you are viewed by your listeners.[63] In a study done to examine the effect of physicians' body language on how they are perceived by their patients, physicians with an open-arm position, who leaned forward while talking and nodded their heads, were viewed more positively.[64] Furthermore, different studies have shown that smiling and eye contact are associated with intelligence and positive perception.[65] So, initiate your communication with a smile, maintain eye contact, and nod your head while leaning forward. Explore other positive body language cues, as these nonverbal messages will help listeners perceive you in a more positive light, and it will help facilitate understanding and perception of your verbal message.

Empathic Communication

Being an empathic speaker means having the capacity to understand and share the feelings and experiences of those to whom you are speaking. In other words, this is simply the ability to imagine yourself in someone else's shoes and share their experience fully as if it were your own. It is a powerful tool that will help you break down barriers when talking to people and form stronger connections. For instance, labeling empathy is one of the greatest skills any negotiator can have, as illustrated by former FBI hostage negotiator and bestselling author Chris Voss in his book *Never Split the Difference*. The way it works is by identifying what the person you are talking to is feeling and then labeling it to show that you understand what they are going through. Interestingly, the value of this skill goes beyond the field of negotiation, and it can be used in any form of communication, whether it is negotiating for a better price on a car, talking with your 5-year-old, or even responding to emails! Nevertheless, you can't be an empathic communicator without first learning how to listen! As author Stephen Covey puts it, "Seek first to understand then to be understood," and in order to do that, you must be actively listening.

A good trick to engage your brain in active listening is to approach each conversation as if you were a reporter interviewing someone on a topic. Thereby, your brain is primed to listen and capture all the information before responding or jumping to conclusions. Notably, psychologist and author Daniel Kahneman in his book *Thinking, Fast and Slow* shows that the brain has a fast and instinctive system that processes emotions and a slow and logical system that deals with rational thought. By focusing on listening rather than responding, your response will be more rational, as you will give the slow and logical system time to process the information and respond instead of giving an emotional, knee-jerk type of response from the fast and instinctive system, which you may regret later on. So, it is important to always slow down before responding, especially if you are emotionally attached to the subject being discussed. Don't let your ego get in the way by thinking that you have heard all you have to hear, as that is the first step toward failed communication. Remember that whatever emotions you may feel, they are a transient rather than permanent state of mind. However, your responses are permanent.

The Audience

Adapting your communication style to your listener is vital for effective communication. For instance, if you are giving a lecture about advances in breast cancer treatment, the language you use and how deep into the details you dive will depend on whether you're presenting it to medical oncologists or students in high school. Furthermore, whenever you are talking about or presenting a subject to people, you should try to imagine your audience's follow-up questions and reactions and tailor your talk based on that. For example, if you are asked to give a presentation about global warming, you shouldn't just prepare a lecture about the causes and dangers of global warming without also capturing the deniers' point of view and their potential counterarguments. This won't just strengthen your argument, as you will be well-prepared for any questions, but it will also help you keep an open and inquisitive mind that is averse to bias.

Final Thoughts

I hope the elite nuggets presented throughout this book benefit you as much as they benefit me both in my personal and professional life, but remember, you have to actually act upon them to gain their benefits! As having knowledge without action is like having a car with a great engine but with no wheels, you are not going anywhere with it!

Without Knowledge, action is useless,
and knowledge without action is futile.

Abu Bakr Siddique

References

1 Claessens, B. J. C.; van Eerde, W.; Rutte, C. G.; Roe, R. A. A Review of the Time Management Literature. *Pers. Rev.* **2007**, *36* (2), 255–276. https://doi.org/10.1108/00483480710726136.

2 Macan, T. H.; Shahani, C.; Dipboye, R. L.; Phillips, A. P. College Students' Time Management: Correlations with Academic Performance and Stress. *J. Educ. Psychol.* **1990**, *82*, 760–768. https://doi.org/10.1037/0022-0663.82.4.760.

3 The-Busy-Persons-Guide-to-the-Done-List.Pdf. https://app.idonethis.com/docs/The-Busy-Persons-Guide-to-the-Done-List.pdf (accessed 2023-01-29).

4 Kruse, K. *How These 'Harvard Questions' Save 8 Hours a Week*. The Good Men Project. https://goodmenproject.com/guy-talk/harvard-questions-save-8-hours-week-fiff/ (accessed 2023-02-02).

5 *Meetings in the Workplace | 2023 Statistics*. LiveCareer. https://www.livecareer.com/resources/careers/planning/workplace-meetings-2022-statistics (accessed 2023-01-29).

[6] Jeong, S.-H.; Hwang, Y. Media Multitasking Effects on Cognitive vs. Attitudinal Outcomes: A Meta-Analysis. *Hum. Commun. Res.* **2016**, *42* (4), 599–618. https://doi.org/10.1111/hcre.12089.

[7] Besson, A.; Tarpin, A.; Flaudias, V.; Brousse, G.; Laporte, C.; Benson, A.; Navel, V.; Bouillon-Minois, J.-B.; Dutheil, F. Smoking Prevalence among Physicians: A Systematic Review and Meta-Analysis. *Int. J. Environ. Res. Public. Health* **2021**, *18* (24), 13328. https://doi.org/10.3390/ijerph182413328.

[8] *The New York Times Test, Goldman Sachs and Greg Smith – Management is a Journey®.* https://managementisajourney.com/the-new-york-times-test-goldman-sachs-and-greg-smith/ (accessed 2023-02-13).

[9] *How to stop negative self-talk.* Mayo Clinic. https://www.mayoclinic.org/healthy-lifestyle/stress-management/in-depth/positive-thinking/art-20043950 (accessed 2023-03-06).

[10] Rosekind, M. R.; Gregory, K. B.; Mallis, M. M.; Brandt, S. L.; Seal, B.; Lerner, D. The Cost of Poor Sleep: Workplace Productivity Loss and Associated Costs. *J. Occup. Environ. Med.* **2010**, *52* (1), 91–98. https://doi.org/10.1097/JOM.0b013e3181c78c30.

[11] Watson, N. F.; Badr, M. S.; Belenky, G.; Bliwise, D. L.; Buxton, O. M.; Buysse, D.; Dinges, D. F.; Gangwisch, J.; Grandner, M. A.; Kushida, C.; Malhotra, R. K.; Martin, J. L.; Patel, S. R.; Quan, S. F.; Tasali, E. Recommended Amount of Sleep for a Healthy Adult: A Joint Consensus Statement of the American Academy of Sleep Medicine and Sleep Research Society. *Sleep* **2015**, *38* (6), 843–844. https://doi.org/10.5665/sleep.4716.

[12] Consensus Conference Panel. Recommended Amount of Sleep for a Healthy Adult: A Joint Consensus Statement of the American Academy of Sleep Medicine and Sleep Research Society. *Sleep* **2015**, *38* (6), 843–844. https://doi.org/10.5665/sleep.4716.

[13] Liu, Y.; Wheaton, A. G.; Chapman, D. P.; Croft, J. B. Sleep Duration and Chronic Diseases among U.S. Adults Age 45 Years and Older: Evidence from the 2010 Behavioral Risk Factor Surveillance System. *Sleep* **2013**, *36* (10), 1421–1427. https://doi.org/10.5665/sleep.3028.

[14] Hogan, C. L.; Mata, J.; Carstensen, L. L. Exercise Holds Immediate Benefits for Affect and Cognition in Younger and Older Adults. *Psychol. Aging* **2013**, *28* (2), 587–594. https://doi.org/10.1037/a0032634.

Samani, A.; Heath, M. Executive-Related Oculomotor Control Is Improved Following a 10-Min Single-Bout of Aerobic Exercise: Evidence from the Antisaccade Task. *Neuropsychologia* **2018**, *108*, 73–81. https://doi.org/10.1016/j.neuropsychologia.2017.11.029.

[15] Coulson, J. C.; McKenna, J.; Field, M. Exercising at Work and Self-reported Work Performance. *Int. J. Workplace Health Manag.* **2008**, *1* (3), 176–197. https://doi.org/10.1108/17538350810926534.

[16] Oppezzo, M.; Schwartz, D. L. Give Your Ideas Some Legs: The Positive Effect of Walking on Creative Thinking. *J. Exp. Psychol. Learn. Mem. Cogn.* **2014**, *40* (4), 1142–1152. https://doi.org/10.1037/a0036577.

[17] Del Giorno, J. M.; Hall, E. E.; O'Leary, K. C.; Bixby, W. R.; Miller, P. C. Cognitive Function during Acute Exercise: A Test of the Transient Hypofrontality Theory. *J. Sport Exerc. Psychol.* **2010**, *32* (3), 312–323. https://doi.org/10.1123/jsep.32.3.312.

[18] *Why Are Habits So Hard to Break?* Duke Today. https://today.duke.edu/2016/01/habits (accessed 2023-03-15).

[19] *Time Spent Using Smartphones (2023 Statistics).* Exploding Topics. https://explodingtopics.com/blog/smartphone-usage-stats (accessed 2023-03-16).

[20] Reznikoff, M.; Domino, G.; Bridges, C.; Honeyman, M. Creative Abilities in Identical and Fraternal Twins. *Behav. Genet.* **1973**, *3* (4), 365–377. https://doi.org/10.1007/BF01070219.

[21] *Componential Theory of Creativity*. HBS Working Knowledge. http://hbswk.hbs.edu/item/componential-theory-of-creativity (accessed 2023-04-04).

[22] Sternberg, R. J. *Handbook of Creativity*; Cambridge University Press, 1999.

[23] Hippel, V.; A, E. Democratizing Innovation. Rochester, NY May 3, 2005. https://papers.ssrn.com/abstract=712763 (accessed 2023-04-09).

[24] *Expert Political Judgment*; 2017.

[25] Root-Bernstein, R. S. Music, Creativity and Scientific Thinking. *Leonardo* **2001**, *34* (1), 63–68. https://doi.org/10.1162/002409401300052532.

Root-Bernstein, R.; Root-Bernstein, M. Artistic Scientists and Scientific Artists: The Link Between Polymathy and Creativity. In *Creativity: From potential to realization*; American Psychological Association: Washington, DC, US, 2004; pp 127–151. https://doi.org/10.1037/10692-008.

Root-Bernstein, R. S.; Bernstein, M.; Garnier, H. Correlations Between Avocations, Scientific Style, Work Habits, and Professional Impact of Scientists. *Creat. Res. J.* **1995**, *8* (2), 115–137. https://doi.org/10.1207/s15326934crj0802_2.

Root-Bernstein, R. S.; Bernstein, M.; Gamier, H. Identification of Scientists Making Long-term, High-impact Contributions, with Notes on Their Methods of Working. *Creat. Res. J.* **1993**, *6* (4), 329–343. https://doi.org/10.1080/10400419309534491.

[26] Isen, A. M.; Daubman, K. A.; Nowicki, G. P. Positive Affect Facilitates Creative Problem Solving. *J. Pers. Soc. Psychol.* **1987**, *52* (6), 1122–1131. https://doi.org/10.1037//0022-3514.52.6.1122.

Estrada, C. A.; Isen, A. M.; Young, M. J. Positive Affect Improves Creative Problem Solving and Influences Reported Source of Practice Satisfaction in Physicians. *Motiv. Emot.* **1994**, *18* (4), 285–299. https://doi.org/10.1007/BF02856470.

[27] Estrada, C. A.; Isen, A. M.; Young, M. J. Positive Affect Improves Creative Problem Solving and Influences Reported Source of Practice Satisfaction in Physicians. *Motiv. Emot.* **1994**, *18* (4), 285–299. https://doi.org/10.1007/BF02856470.

[28] Isen, A. M.; Daubman, K. A.; Nowicki, G. P. Positive Affect Facilitates Creative Problem Solving. *J. Pers. Soc. Psychol.* **1987**, *52* (6), 1122–1131. https://doi.org/10.1037//0022-3514.52.6.1122.

[29] Kashdan, T. B.; Disabato, D. J.; Goodman, F. R.; Naughton, C. The Five Dimensions of Curiosity. *Harvard Business Review.* September 1, 2018. https://hbr.org/2018/09/the-five-dimensions-of-curiosity (accessed 2023-04-17).

[30] Robson, D. *Awe: The "little earthquake" that could free your mind.* https://www.bbc.com/worklife/article/20220103-awe-the-little-earthquake-that-could-free-your-mind (accessed 2023-04-17).

[31] Zedelius, C. M.; Protzko, J.; Broadway, J. M.; Schooler, J. W. What Types of Daydreaming Predict Creativity? Laboratory and Experience Sampling Evidence. *Psychol. Aesthet. Creat. Arts* **2021**, *15*, 596–611. https://doi.org/10.1037/aca0000342.

[32] Ellwood, S.; Pallier, G.; Snyder, A.; Gallate, J. The Incubation Effect: Hatching a Solution? *Creat. Res. J.* **2009**, *21* (1), 6–14. https://doi.org/10.1080/10400410802633368.

Gilhooly, K. J.; Georgiou, G.; Devery, U. Incubation and Creativity: Do Something Different. *Think. Reason.* **2013**, *19* (2), 137–149. https://doi.org/10.1080/13546783.2012.749812.

33 Rominger, C.; Fink, A.; Weber, B.; Papousek, I.; Schwerdtfeger, A. R. Everyday Bodily Movement Is Associated with Creativity Independently from Active Positive Affect: A Bayesian Mediation Analysis Approach. *Sci. Rep.* **2020**, *10* (1), 11985. https://doi.org/10.1038/s41598-020-68632-9.

34 Oppezzo, M.; Schwartz, D. L. Give Your Ideas Some Legs: The Positive Effect of Walking on Creative Thinking. *J. Exp. Psychol. Learn. Mem. Cogn.* **2014**, *40* (4), 1142–1152. https://doi.org/10.1037/a0036577.

35 Slepian, M. L.; Ambady, N. Fluid Movement and Creativity. *J. Exp. Psychol. Gen.* **2012**, *141*, 625–629. https://doi.org/10.1037/a0027395.

36 Lewis, P. A.; Knoblich, G.; Poe, G. How Memory Replay in Sleep Boosts Creative Problem-Solving. *Trends Cogn. Sci.* **2018**, *22*, 491–503. https://doi.org/10.1016/j.tics.2018.03.009.

Cai, D. J.; Mednick, S. A.; Harrison, E. M.; Kanady, J. C.; Mednick, S. C. REM, Not Incubation, Improves Creativity by Priming Associative Networks. *Proc. Natl. Acad. Sci.* **2009**, *106* (25), 10130–10134. https://doi.org/10.1073/pnas.0900271106.

[37] Ritter, S. M.; Strick, M.; Bos, M. W.; van Baaren, R. B.; Dijksterhuis, A. Good Morning Creativity: Task Reactivation during Sleep Enhances Beneficial Effect of Sleep on Creative Performance. *J. Sleep Res.* **2012**, *21* (6), 643–647. https://doi.org/10.1111/j.1365-2869.2012.01006.x.

[38] *HM, the Man with No Memory | Psychology Today.* https://www.psychologytoday.com/us/blog/trouble-in-mind/201201/hm-the-man-no-memory (accessed 2023-04-20).

[39] Maguire, E. A.; Gadian, D. G.; Johnsrude, I. S.; Good, C. D.; Ashburner, J.; Frackowiak, R. S.; Frith, C. D. Navigation-Related Structural Change in the Hippocampi of Taxi Drivers. *Proc. Natl. Acad. Sci. U. S. A.* **2000**, *97* (8), 4398–4403. https://doi.org/10.1073/pnas.070039597.

[40] Willis, S. L.; Tennstedt, S. L.; Marsiske, M.; Ball, K.; Elias, J.; Koepke, K. M.; Morris, J. N.; Rebok, G. W.; Unverzagt, F. W.; Stoddard, A. M.; Wright, E. Long-Term Effects of Cognitive Training on Everyday Functional Outcomes in Older Adults. *JAMA J. Am. Med. Assoc.* **2006**, *296* (23), 2805. https://doi.org/10.1001/jama.296.23.2805.

Anderson, K.; Grossberg, G. T. Brain Games to Slow Cognitive Decline in Alzheimer's Disease. *J. Am. Med. Dir. Assoc.* **2014**, *15* (8), 536–537. https://doi.org/10.1016/j.jamda.2014.04.014.

Karp, A.; Paillard-Borg, S.; Wang, H.-X.; Silverstein, M.; Winblad, B.; Fratiglioni, L. Mental, Physical and Social Components in Leisure Activities Equally Contribute to Decrease Dementia Risk. *Dement. Geriatr. Cogn. Disord.* **2006**, *21* (2), 65–73. https://doi.org/10.1159/000089919.

Wilson, R. S.; Scherr, P. A.; Schneider, J. A.; Tang, Y.; Bennett, D. A. Relation of Cognitive Activity to Risk of Developing Alzheimer Disease. *Neurology* **2007**, *69* (20), 1911–1920. https://doi.org/10.1212/01.wnl.0000271087.67782.cb.

[41] Willis, S. L.; Tennstedt, S. L.; Marsiske, M.; Ball, K.; Elias, J.; Koepke, K. M.; Morris, J. N.; Rebok, G. W.; Unverzagt, F. W.; Stoddard, A. M.; Wright, E. Long-Term Effects of Cognitive Training on Everyday Functional Outcomes in Older Adults. *JAMA J. Am. Med. Assoc.* **2006**, *296* (23), 2805. https://doi.org/10.1001/jama.296.23.2805.

[42] Wilson, R. S.; Scherr, P. A.; Schneider, J. A.; Tang, Y.; Bennett, D. A. Relation of Cognitive Activity to Risk of Developing Alzheimer Disease. *Neurology* **2007**, *69* (20), 1911–1920. https://doi.org/10.1212/01.wnl.0000271087.67782.cb.

[43] Henkel, L. A. Point-and-Shoot Memories: The Influence of Taking Photos on Memory for a Museum Tour. *Psychol. Sci.* **2014**, *25* (2), 396–402. https://doi.org/10.1177/0956797613504438.

[44] Beşoluk, Ş.; Önder, İ.; Deveci, İ. Morningness-Eveningness Preferences and Academic Achievement of University Students. *Chronobiol. Int.* **2011**, *28* (2), 118–125. https://doi.org/10.3109/07420528.2010.540729

[45] Umejima, K.; Ibaraki, T.; Yamazaki, T.; Sakai, K. L. Paper Notebooks vs. Mobile Devices: Brain Activation Differences During Memory Retrieval. *Front. Behav. Neurosci.* **2021**, *15*.

[46] NW, 1615 L. St; Washington, S. 800; Inquiries, D. 20036 U.-419-4300 | M.-857-8562 | F.-419-4372 | M. *Public Knowledge of Current Affairs Little Changed by News and Information Revolutions*. Pew Research Center - U.S. Politics & Policy. https://www.pewresearch.org/politics/2007/04/15/public-knowledge-of-current-affairs-little-changed-by-news-and-information-revolutions/ (accessed 2023-04-24).

[47] Wanzer, M. B.; Frymier, A. B.; Irwin, J. An Explanation of the Relationship between Instructor Humor and Student Learning: Instructional Humor Processing Theory. *Commun. Educ.* **2010**, *59* (1), 1–18. https://doi.org/10.1080/03634520903367238.

Garner, R. L. Humor in Pedagogy: How Ha-Ha Can Lead to Aha! *Coll. Teach.* **2006**, *54* (1), 177–180. https://doi.org/10.3200/CTCH.54.1.177-180.

[48] Rayner, K.; Schotter, E. R.; Masson, M. E. J.; Potter, M. C.; Treiman, R. So Much to Read, So Little Time: How Do We Read, and Can Speed Reading Help? *Psychol. Sci. Public Interest* **2016**, *17* (1), 4–34. https://doi.org/10.1177/1529100615623267.

[49] Rayner, K.; Schotter, E. R.; Masson, M. E. J.; Potter, M. C.; Treiman, R. So Much to Read, So Little Time: How Do We Read, and Can Speed Reading Help? *Psychol. Sci. Public Interest* **2016**, *17* (1), 4–34. https://doi.org/10.1177/1529100615623267.

[50] *Learn to Read Faster – Stop "Regressing."* Spreeder. https://www.spreeder.com/learn-to-read-faster-stop-regressing/ (accessed 2023-04-27).

Oppong, T. *Want to Read More Books Without Losing Comprehension? Learn to Resist Regression.* Thrive Global. https://community.thriveglobal.com/reading-resisting-regression/ (accessed 2023-04-27).

[51] Inhoff, A. W.; Kim, A.; Radach, R. Regressions during Reading. *Vision* **2019**, *3* (3), 35. https://doi.org/10.3390/vision3030035.

[52] Aleksić, V.; Stanković, N.; Papic, M.; Bešić, C. The Evaluation of Using Mind Maps in Teaching. *Tech. Technol. Educ. Manag.* **2011**, *6*, 337–343.

Malekzadeh, B.; Bayat, A. The Effect of Mind Mapping Strategy on Comprehending Implicit Information in EFL Reading Texts.

Rezapour-Nasrabad, R. Mind Map Learning Technique: An Educational Interactive Approach. *Int. J. Pharm. Res.* **2019**, *11*, 1593–1597.

[53] Aleksić, V.; Stanković, N.; Papic, M.; Bešić, C. The Evaluation of Using Mind Maps in Teaching. *Tech. Technol. Educ. Manag.* **2011**, *6*, 337–343.

[54] Malekzadeh, B.; Bayat, A. The Effect of Mind Mapping Strategy on Comprehending Implicit Information in EFL Reading Texts.

[55] Blocki, J.; Komanduri, S.; Cranor, L.; Datta, A. Spaced Repetition and Mnemonics Enable Recall of Multiple Strong Passwords. In *Proceedings 2015 Network and Distributed System Security Symposium*; 2015. https://doi.org/10.14722/ndss.2015.23094.

Settles, B.; Meeder, B. A Trainable Spaced Repetition Model for Language Learning. In *Proceedings of the 54th Annual Meeting of the Association for Computational Linguistics (Volume 1: Long Papers)*; Association for Computational Linguistics: Berlin, Germany, 2016; pp 1848–1858. https://doi.org/10.18653/v1/P16-1174.

Teninbaum, G. H. Spaced Repetition: A Method for Learning More Law in Less Time. *J. High Technol. Law* **2016**, *17*, 273. Ausubel, D. P.; Youssef, M. The Effect of Spaced Repetition on Meaningful Retention. *J. Gen. Psychol.* **1965**, *73* (1), 147–150. https://doi.org/10.1080/00221309.1965.9711263.

Kang, S. H. K. Spaced Repetition Promotes Efficient and Effective Learning: Policy Implications for Instruction. *Policy Insights Behav. Brain Sci.* **2016**, *3* (1), 12–19. https://doi.org/10.1177/2372732215624708.

Zirkle, D. M.; Ellis, A. K. Effects of Spaced Repetition on Long-Term Map Knowledge Recall. *J. Geogr.* **2010**, *109* (5), 201–206. https://doi.org/10.1080/00221341.2010.504780.

[56] Zirkle, D. M.; Ellis, A. K. Effects of Spaced Repetition on Long-Term Map Knowledge Recall. *J. Geogr.* **2010**, *109* (5), 201–206. https://doi.org/10.1080/00221341.2010.504780.

[57] Karpicke, J. D.; Bauernschmidt, A. Spaced Retrieval: Absolute Spacing Enhances Learning Regardless of Relative Spacing. *J. Exp. Psychol. Learn. Mem. Cogn.* **2011**, *37* (5), 1250–1257. https://doi.org/10.1037/a0023436.

[58] Arnold, K. M.; McDermott, K. B. Free Recall Enhances Subsequent Learning. *Psychon. Bull. Rev.* **2013**, *20* (3), 507–513. https://doi.org/10.3758/s13423-012-0370-3.

[59] Rummer, R.; Schweppe, J.; Gerst, K.; Wagner, S. Is Testing a More Effective Learning Strategy than Note-Taking? *J. Exp. Psychol. Appl.* **2017**, *23*, 293–300. https://doi.org/10.1037/xap0000134.

[60] Campitelli, G.; Gobet, F. Deliberate Practice: Necessary But Not Sufficient. *Curr. Dir. Psychol. Sci.* **2011**, *20* (5), 280–285. https://doi.org/10.1177/0963721411421922.

[61] Tversky, A.; Kahneman, D. The Framing of Decisions and the Psychology of Choice. *Science* **1981**, *211* (4481), 453–458. https://doi.org/10.1126/science.7455683.

[62] Shapira, A. Breathing Is the Key to Persuasive Public Speaking. *Harvard Business Review*. June 30, 2015. https://hbr.org/2015/06/breathing-is-the-key-to-persuasive-public-speaking (accessed 2023-05-16).

[63] McGinley, H.; LeFevre, R.; McGinley, P. The Influence of a Communicator's Body Position on Opinion Change in Others. *J. Pers. Soc. Psychol.* **1975**, *31*, 686–690. https://doi.org/10.1037/0022-3514.31.4.686.

[64] Harrigan, J. A.; Rosenthal, R. Physicians' H]Ead and Body Positions as Determinants of Perceived Rapport. *J. Appl. Soc. Psychol.* **1983**, *13* (6), 496–509. https://doi.org/10.1111/j.1559-1816.1983.tb02332.x.

[65] Lau, S. The Effect of Smiling on Person Perception. *J. Soc. Psychol.* **1982**, *117* (1), 63–67. https://doi.org/10.1080/00224545.1982.9713408.

Murphy, N. A. Appearing Smart: The Impression Management of Intelligence, Person Perception Accuracy, and Behavior in Social Interaction. *Pers. Soc. Psychol. Bull.* **2007**, *33* (3), 325–339. https://doi.org/10.1177/0146167206294871.